Randi Ettner (signature)

CONFESSIONS OF A GENDER DEFENDER

A Psychologist's Reflections on Life Among the Transgendered

Randi Ettner, Ph.D.

CHICAGO SPECTRUM PRESS
EVANSTON, IL 60201

©1996 by Randi Ettner

 CHICAGO SPECTRUM PRESS
1571 SHERMAN AVENUE
EVANSTON, IL 60201

Printed in the U.S.A.
10 9 8 7 6 5 4 3 2 1

ISBN: 1-886094-51-9

This book is dedicated to my aunt, Dr. Leah Cahan Schaefer, who blew a dream into my soul when I was five years old and nurtured it ever after.

NON CREDO

To those who did not think this book would succeed, and especially to the literary "giant" of an editor who referred to the transgendered as "yucky," thank you for giving me the drive to prove you wrong.

In the words of comedian and screenwriter Tim Kazurinsky: "You can't judge a man until you've walked a mile in his high heels."

TABLE OF CONTENTS

ACKNOWLEDGMENTS

I am so grateful!

First, I give thanks and my undying love and admiration to my husband, Fred. His willingness to buck the system and treat people as the unique human beings they are is a rarity today in medicine. I thank him for his support and love, and for providing the stability that allowed me to do "outreach" while he cared for our children. Fred, you are the most powerful medicine man I have ever known and a true healer of souls and bodies. Thanks to Annelise and Joseph Oliver, my darling children, who have taught me more than any professors, colleagues, or institutions.

To Rita Mendelsohn, who read, reread, and supported me, as always. Thank you for teaching me about persistence, and for your incredible love.

To the late Robert S. Mendelsohn, beloved friend, mentor, and physician, who taught me to question everything, and whose first book, *Confessions of a Medical Heretic*, was the inspiration for this book.

To Barbara Kohn, who gave me literary license to "misquote" her liberally, and yet still remains the epitome of friendship.

To Samantha Thomas, for her many skills, her assistance, love, support, humor, protection, and loyalty. It would not be possible to do this work without her.

To my parents, Fay and Sydney Cahan, for their unconditional love and support, without which I would have surely ended up to be a "gangster's moll" as my high school algebra teacher predicted.

To my big brothers, Eric and Michael Cahan, who continue to protect, counsel and care for me.

To James and Vera Chatz, and Ellen and Anne O'Connell, for all your love, support, and assistance. Thank you for being my family.

To Eleanore and Louis Altman, who tirelessly offer support to families of the transgendered, and single-handedly move mountains. You are the kindest people I know.

To Amber Lightfoot, for believing in avatars, and to The Standing People.

To my literary agent, Susan Golomb, with gratitude for everything.

To Eugene A. Schrang, M.D., I give my gratitude and love for everything you have done.

To Nat Silverman, for your friendship, public relations expertise, and I confess, mostly for the laughs.

And most importantly, to all my clients and transgendered friends who shared their journeys with me. It is a privilege to be permitted to participate in your lives. Thank you.

INTRODUCTION

"Gender is the most misunderstood topic of our times." Freud made a similar statement over 70 years ago and Dr. Ettner reminds us that it is still true. In spite of gender's mysteries and voyeuristic possibilities, Dr. Ettner goes far in helping us to close the imposing empathy gap that inevitably exists between sex-gender congruent and incongruent persons. For that reason alone, this delightful book should be read in one sitting by anyone who comes into contact with transgendered persons—helping professionals, family members, friends, clergy, civil servants, and "significant others."

Dr. Ettner brings to bear two decades of clinical experience that support her, and my belief that transsexuals are born, not "made." I would like to be able to criticize the author for compiling a sensationalized, *Jerry Springeresque* collection of the most outrageous, unrepresentative stories of gender-conflicted persons she could dredge up. I cannot. The stories here are pedestrian to those of us who have pursued a similar professional calling. They are all too commonplace, with different names and different faces and comparably tragic or triumphant outcomes. In her chapters, Dr. Ettner demonstrates the importance of being both a sensitive clinician and an observant researcher if helping professionals want to best assist transgendered persons. Her systematic observation of height differences between post-operative male-to-female transsexuals and non-transgendered men serves as one such example that may have important clinical implications.

"Gender defenders" such as Randi Ettner are often ostracized by many of their professional peers who were, after all, raised with the same biases and prejudices regarding "gender benders" as society as large. Professional school education (medicine, psychology, social work, etc.) rarely does anything to change this harsh reality. Dr. Ettner poignantly demonstrates the disdain of other professionals toward our work, e.g., the cosmetic plastic surgeon who doesn't consider SRS "valid" surgery but who has no ethical (or financial) constraints against "tummy tucks" and face lifts. I congratulate Dr. Ettner for her courage in publishing her experiences.

Dr. Ettner reminds us that to provide care and understanding for gender-conflicted persons often requires novel approaches to making oneself available to a stigmatized, often fearful population. These creative approaches may include meeting in basements, gay bars, church annexes, and Holiday Inn rooms, all of which I have done, just as Dr. Ettner discloses. Gender defenders are proactive, unconventional, and mobile!

In summary, this book is well organized in that the chapters blend into each other like the many shades of gender expression. It is authentic, nonsensational, self-disclosing, and humorous. A single-session reading is recommended to fully experience the bridging of the empathy gap between those trapped in a single gender and those who are more flexibly endowed.

–George R. Brown, M.D.

Associate Chairman, Dept. of Psychiatry,
East Tennessee State University,

Chief of Psychiatry, Mountain Home VAMC,
Johnson City, Tennessee, and

Board of Directors, Harry Benjamin
International Gender Dysphoria Association

AUTHOR'S NOTE

This is my story. I share it, in the hope of creating a climate of acceptance. This is not meant to be a textbook on gender identity disorders. The reader who is interested in more information is referred to the references at the back of this book.

MEDIA ATTENTION
The Prying Game

This is no coincidence. At the precise moment that "The Crying Game" was nominated for an Academy Award, I was catapulted from simple psychologist to dinner guest extraordinaire. Everyone wanted "my take" on the film. Did I really move about effortlessly in this netherworld of weirdos? Did my patients look like Jaye Davidson, absolutely convincing, but really guys?

A reporter from a local paper has arranged to interview my husband and me about a column we write on pregnancy and childbirth. She arrives, but she isn't interested in talking about pregnancy. She wants exotica. We try to steer her back to the topic at hand. She writes a story about transsexualism.

There is an incredible fascination about the transsexual phenomenon. Gender is the most misunderstood subject of our times. I have sought to clear up some mis-

19

conceptions. In the process I have learned a thing or two about the media.

An article appears in the *New York Times*. It is about gender identity disorders in children. It takes the position that many gender problems in children can be cured with certain therapies. It quotes a few different experts. Oprah Winfrey's producers have decided to do a program about this. They call me and ask me my opinion. "What would you say if you were on?" they ask.

Imagine, if you can a young child who feels innately that she is a little girl but in fact, is not. She tells her mother, "But Mommy, I'm really a girl." The mother says, "Don't you ever say that again. You are a boy and you will always be a boy." Unfortunately, few parents can tolerate the concept of having a child who is transgendered.

In fact, our whole society is guilty of this intolerance. We are very insistent that there are only two clear-cut genders. Our commitment to the belief in this binary system is reflected in our language and in the law. But as many as four percent of all births are intersexed (both male and female organs are present) according to Dr. Anne Fausto-Sterling, developmental geneticist.. In other societies people who are transgendered are revered or worshiped. In Burma, for instance, men who dress like women play an important part in the spiritual life of the Burmese. Moreover, there is a great deal of fluidity in Burma, unlike in our society where we are dedicated to categorizing. Clinicians like myself who work with gender people speak about primary and secondary transsexuals, the transvestic transsexual, and other diagnostic subgroups. Our training encourages us to put people in these gender pigeonholes.

But let's return to our prototypical three-year old transsexual who feels herself to be a girl and yet is a natal boy. The parents, as noted, don't tolerate any "sissy" behavior. Fairly soon, typically in middle childhood, the child learns to shut up about "her" real feelings and to bury this painful secret inside.

However, when no one is home, the child will put on the mother's or sister's clothes and feel the congruence of looking and feeling the same. This feeling will be short-lived, for the child must never reveal to any one this most innermost thought that *he is really a she.*

Recently, a 51 year old man, "Jake," came to see me from a small town in Indiana. He was severely depressed and claimed to be suicidal. He had been gender dysphoric all his life. When he was twelve, he told his family doctor about his feelings. The doctor said, "You're crazy and should be in a mental hospital. But since I like your parents, I'm going to just pretend we never had this conversation." Well Jake never told another living soul about his condition. He married, had a son, joined the marines, and grew increasingly depressed. When his son, a pilot, died, he felt that he had nothing to live for. He came to see me, thinking, "It's this or suicide."

A minute dose of female hormones now enables Jake to live comfortably as a man. He will take these hormones for the rest of his life.

Yes, many young children experiment with trying on clothes of the opposite sex. Few, however, express the persistent wish to *be* the opposite sex. These children go to sleep praying that they will awaken and be miraculously transformed into the opposite gender. One of my

21

transsexual patients describes the horror of such a child-hood by saying, "Life's a bitch. Then you become one."

"But they outgrow this!" Oprah's producer insists.

"Do they?" I ask," Or does this reemerge at puberty? I am treating people from all over the country who did not outgrow this."

"I don't think we'll do this show, after all," the producer says. "We don't want to alarm parents."

BETTER DEAD THAN READ

Carl is a thirty-year-old white male who has been taken to the hospital by police after throwing bottles at his mother and threatening to kill himself. He has been admitted to the psychiatric unit, and is undergoing evaluation for organic brain syndrome. Five years ago, while washing windows, Carl fell five stories and hit a concrete sidewalk. He was awarded a $600,000 settlement. He went to Atlantic City, spent $100,000 drinking and gambling, and came home to get more money. A huge fight ensued with his mother, at which point the police intervened. The remaining money was put in an irrevocable trust.

≡

It is Tuesday morning. I have just dropped the kids at school when I hear my office phone ring. I answer, and recognize the voice of a psychiatrist I know on the other end. Dr. Coughlin tells me he is referring a patient to me who has sustained a severe head injury in an accident some years back, and whom he is treating for substance abuse and bipolar affective disorder. The patient will soon be released from the hospital.

"Why me?" I ask incredulously. "I don't specialize in neuropsychology, and I don't deal with substance abuse either." Thanks, but no thanks. Wrong number.

"The patient wants to wear woman's clothing. I can't deal with this" he confesses.

"Send him to me as soon as he's out. I'll be happy to co-manage this case with you. Oh, . . . and thanks for the referral!"

Hormones have a profound effect on the brain. A person can induce a male monkey to care for an orphan monkey baby by injecting estrogens. The adult male monkey will became a pseudo-caretaker, and engage in maternal behaviors.

The human brain develops rapidly before birth. Effects of hormones on the brain in utero, can cause lifelong behavioral sequelae. In the gender dysphoric individual, giving feminizing hormones generally induces a sense of well-being. For many, it acts like an antidepressant, quieting the agitation of "being in the wrong body." It is similar to the experience of many postmenopausal women who, when placed on estrogen replacement regimens, suddenly feel restored to their previous levels of well-being.

I, like many others who specialize in gender issues, believe that gender dysphoria may have a biological basis. Theoretically, the brain may have become "feminized" early on in the fetal development. Normally, the morphology of the body follows suit. In rare cases, however, the body develops in opposition to the brain, and the person may be born with a feminized brain in a male body, (or a masculinized brain in a female body).

A simple analogy is the individual who is born with two different eye colors. In most cases, the genetic information translates to produce two eyes that are identical in color. In some rare cases, however, eye color is not bilaterally symmetric.

Gender conditions, like transsexualism, may be birth errors. The individual comes into the world with this condition, and leaves the world with this condition. Nothing can cure this. It never goes away. In an attempt to "cure" themselves, most male-to-female transsexuals experience a "flight into hypermasculinity," including marrying, jumping out of planes, or joining the military. Ultimately these attempts fail. The gender dysphoric person becomes increasingly depressed. Without treatment, many commit suicide.

One year has passed. Carl is now Carla. She is sitting in my office wearing a pink sweater, jeans, and carrying a purse. She is calm. She is happy. She no longer takes psychotropic drugs for bipolar disorder. She no longer takes medication to help control her angry impulses. She no longer abuses alcohol. She is stable.

Carla is wearing makeup which is actually rather garish looking. You can see tiny breasts forcing a contour in her sweater. They are the result of the estrogenic hormones she has been taking. She is a tad peculiar looking, like a woman who might be of slightly below normal intelligence. Nevertheless, she has a sense of humor and enough insight and confidence to laugh at herself. She is studying computer programming and dreaming of sex reassignment surgery.

Today Carla and I are talking about her childhood. She is the adopted child of religious parents. Like most transsexuals, she has perceived herself to be a girl in the wrong body as far back as she can recall. Unlike other transsexuals, she has a hard time expressing this, because she has intellectual deficits. She speaks very slowly, as though she is searching for words. She has dressed in girls' clothing ever since childhood. In fact, she laughingly recalls, that on the day of her disastrous accident, she was taken by ambulance to the emergency room. She arrived unconscious, wearing a bra and panties beneath her outergarments.

Carla's mother phones. She is enraged at me. I have encouraged her son to dress like a girl. She has forbidden him to ever enter the church where she works, for fear of embarrassing her. Furthermore, the mother has no intention of paying me for my services. If I want to, I can try to get the money out of the irrevocable trust fund.

There it is again. Parents can accept a child who is a murderer more easily than a child who is a transsexual.

I phone the psychiatrist, Dr. Coughlin.

"He is insisting that I refer to him as Carla." he complains.

"Try to be flexible" I say coaxingly. "Call her Carla."

"My idea of being flexible is working evenings."

The family is the basic unit of society. By extension, the family's reactions to having a transsexual member is a barometer of society's reaction to this phenomenon. Most often, the nuclear family reacts by withdrawing membership and its privileges from the individual who dares to cross the inviolable gender borderline. Having crossed that line, the offending offspring is banished to an emotional Siberia, a twentieth-century leper colony. They are no longer welcome in their family of origin—not even at Christmas.

Every pregnant woman imbues her unborn child with God's gifts. The idealized child is limitless . . . beautiful, brilliant, and a statesman, to boot. Only with birth and the months thereafter does the expectant mother shed some of the more grandiose fantasies. Perhaps he won't be a great athlete, she concedes, judging from his inability to crawl at nine months, but he'll be a genius—better still. With every developmental milestone vaulted and every compliment received, the new parents bask in the narcissistic glow of having created this extraordinary and totally unique individual.

In our society, there is a deeply ingrained belief that the parents are ultimately responsible for shaping the development, character, and adult nature of their offspring. A nation of American mothers, with worn out copies of Dr. Spock at their night tables, raised their children according to prevailing pediatric wisdom.

This notion that the parents were responsible for the child's success or failure in life was further broadened by a tradition of psychoanalytic thought that portrayed the mother as the transmitter of psychological diseases. If a child were diagnosed as schizophrenic, the mother was considered to be "schizophrenegenic," a term that meant she was alternately accepting and rejecting—which drove the child crazy. Similarly, mothers of autistic children were long thought to be cold and emotionally withholding.

The influence of psychoanalytic interpretations waned with the rise of technological capacities to isolate possible biologic antecedents for conditions such as hyperactivity, schizophrenia, and the like. Nevertheless, the notion that "the apple doesn't fall far from the tree" remains the cornerstone of familial mythology. "My son the doctor" was the phrase that elevated immigrant women to a previously unattainable status among their peers. Having a successful adult child is tantamount to being successful. The obvious implication is that one has spent a lifetime parenting in an exemplary way, and that the fruits of one's labors are now evident. "As ye sow, so shall ye reap."

Few things are as devastating to parents as learning that their child is a transsexual. The narcissistic injury in having a child who wants to change genders is beyond description. Parents can accept a child who is a criminal more easily than a child who is transgendered. Our society reinforces this intolerance by constantly bombarding us with images of the transsexual as a bizarre, marginal deviate with multiple pathologies. We are witness, almost on a daily basis, to a media barrage of unparalleled sensationalism. Over and over again, day in and day out I am asked, "Why would anyone want to change their sex?" It is the litmus test of insanity. The transsexual is a leper in modern society, and the parents are considered to be the breeders of the contagion.

It is no coincidence that the transsexual is the only minority group that has no political lobby whatsoever. They are specifically excluded from the Americans with Disabilities Act, whose express purpose is to protect individuals from discrimination. Politicians are people. They harbor the same prejudices as the constituents they represent. They echo the sentiments of the public and transform these sentiments into law. To them, the transsexual is a deranged creature, at best. At worst, the transsexual is an evil opponent of God, not worthy of consideration, let alone medical or legal protection.

It is within this context of contempt that parents struggle to incorporate the "information" that their child is a transsexual. With no support, no information, and no compassion, the parents, not surprisingly fail. They internalize the shame of having failed on such a large scale, on all counts. Overwhelmed by pain and confusion, having to "rewrite" their entire personal history, most disengage from the child. They behave as though the child, now an adult, is dead.

One patient of mine, a twenty-two year old, still young enough to desperately need a mother, would drive to her mother's home and ring the bell. The mother, seeing her at the door, would hide upstairs and draw the curtains. Others, sadly, have no contact whatsoever with their parents. Years later, they learn of their parents' death only by reading the obituaries.

BEGINNINGS

T homas came to my office looking exactly like an engineer — a pocketful of pencils, a watch that did logarithms, and a receding hairline. I guessed his age to be about thirty-six. I asked him why he had come an hour's drive to see me. There must be psychologists in his home town. "I have a psychologist" he said, "and a psychiatrist. I need a specialist. I'm a transsexual."

"What makes you think you're a transsexual?" I asked.

"Well, for instance, the other day I'm walking down the street with my business partner, and we see this really attractive woman. My buddy is thinking 'I'd like to jump on her bones.' I'm thinking, 'cute shoes!'"

In the late 1970s, I became the first psychology intern in the Department of Psychiatry at Cook County Hospital in Chicago. Since there was no existing position, my rotations were chosen on an "as needed" basis.

One of my first assignments was to be a co-therapist for a group of transsexuals. I had never seen, or even heard of a transsexual, although I had a vague notion that someone named Christine Jorgenson had changed her sex. My supervisor prepared me as we walked to the outpatient clinic: "Remember these are all really men. They are very disturbed individuals who think they can change what's inside by changing their outside. Nevertheless, many of them will have surgery performed right here at County."

Nothing could have prepared me for that first encounter. I was led into a room of about eighteen women, some of whom were absolutely gorgeous. They could have been models. (Later I found out that many were.) I sat there for half an hour unable to say anything. I just kept repeating over and over to myself "All these women have penises. All these women have penises."

Now, nearly two decades later, I'm convinced that the cognitive dissonance that arises from this condition is one reason that so few clinicians can work with these individuals. It is disruptive to have two competing beliefs operating in consciousness simultaneously. The visual cues lead to one conclusion, but the clinician's internal voice refutes it.

≋

THOMAS' JOURNAL

I just didn't know where to begin to find the help I needed. I called Dr. Renee Richards after reading her autobiography. She didn't want to talk to me, but she referred me to Dr. Leah Schaefer, a New York City psychologist who specializes in gender. While I would have flown to New York, if I had to, she told me she had a colleague who practices in my state.

> First Meeting with Dr. Ettner:
> Wednesday, June 23, 1993, 2:17 p.m.
> This is the beginning of the rest of my life. . .

Dr. Ettner knows the torment that I've faced all my life, and she is ready and willing to help me become real. This is not something that can be accomplished overnight. I know that it will take months to become feminized by the hormones. It will take even longer to learn the arcana of womanhood. Even so, I want to start the "life test" by January 1994, with reassignment surgery following one year later. Total process time to become real: 18 to 20 months. THE JOURNEY HAS BEGUN!

I felt more than a little panicky on the way to see Dr. Ettner this afternoon. It was especially bad on the expressway. On the way home, I chose not to avoid the expressway. I was so relaxed, it was almost spooky. This is right. This is good.

> Wednesday, June 30, 1993
> Second meeting with Dr. Ettner

Arrived at Dr. Ettner's office at 2:40 pm — ten minutes late. With car problems, the flood and the horrendous traffic because of all the closed roads in the county, I'm glad I was able to make it at all. I would have walked to get there, if I had to. We continued our discussion of what lies ahead. I am very eager to get on with it. I told Dr. Ettner about telling my ex-wife about the transition last Sunday. Dr. Ettner was pleased that it went so well and that I have an important early addition to my support team. My parents are next, then my closest business associates: George, Jim, and Tony.

My first full day on hormones will be my 36th birthday. Happy, happy birthday!!

Gave Dr. Ettner my new name: Samantha Renee Thomas.

Samantha means "requested of God." When I was little, around four or so, my dad nicknamed me "Sam." I felt safe when he called me Sam, because Sam never got beaten. Tom was beaten a lot, usually with a leather belt. When dad called me "Sam" it meant that he was in a good mood and I was safe. I pretended that "Sam" was short for Samantha, but I never mentioned that to anyone. I always wanted to be Samantha.

Renee means "reborn." In addition to the significance of its meaning, Renee is a tribute to Dr. Richards who cleared a path for me.

Thomas means "twin." A link to my past affirming the continuation of self. A reference to my dual nature. I cherish Tom for his perseverance and sacrifice.

Thursday, July 1, 1993

Met with Dr. Wetherbe. I asked her if she would be willing to write the second opinion when the time came. She said, "I am convinced that this is the only way to resolve this major conflict in your life. I'm just glad you're letting me be a part of it. Of course I'll write it."

We talked about my relationships with Evangelical Christians and how the transition would affect them. Evangelicals have a way of shooting the wounded. (It makes them feel holy, although it is, in truth, the exact opposite.) If they can't accept my transition, I will simply disassociate myself from them. It would be their loss, not mine. This applies to any negative influence I may face.

The entire law is summed up in a single command: love your neighbor as yourself. If you keep on biting and devouring each other, watch out or you will be destroyed by each other. (Galatians 5:14,15)

I am not accusing God of making a mistake. This is a challenge for me — the same as any challenge anyone faces. God, in His mercy, has provided me with a way to answer this challenge in the most positive way. I will be victorious. Anyone who can't see that, or refuses to see that, has a more serious problem than I do.

The clinical term is gender dysphoria. The Diagnostic and Statistical Manual of Psychiatric Disorders (DSM) defines it as a persistent feeling that one's true gender does not match one's physical body.

In order to establish a diagnosis of gender identity disorder, this feeling must persist over time. It is often accompanied by the desire or compulsion to cross-dress. In the most severe cases, the individual desires sex-reassignment surgery to completely alter the physiognomy, including reconstruction of the genitals.

Now, one year later, Thomas has undergone hormone treatment and is attempting to "transition." He looks like a rather heavy, unattractive woman, but a protruding Adam's apple and a masculine voice make him easy to "read." Thomas is now referring to himself as Samantha and I too have switched to the female name—not an easy shift for me at this point either.

"Samantha, I'm writing a book about transsexualism and want permission to include your journal excerpts."

"What are you going to call it?" she asked. "Everything you want to know about sex change but don't have the balls to ask?"

The next day an envelope arrives at my door. A note was stuck to the journal entries:

> Randi-
>
> *I gave you some of the early ones. Back when I was happy and optimistic. Before people started telling me how ugly and unfeminine I am. Before my business went kaflooie. Before some friends proved themselves to be not friends.*
>
> *Oh well—*
>
> *It ain't over till I (the fat lady) sing, and I ain't singin' 'til I get into alto range! (Soprano is a little too much to hope for).*
>
> *Love, Sam*

The desire to change one's gender can be so compelling for some, that it has been referred to in the medical literature as "the transsexual imperative." Some gender dysphoric individuals such as Thomas, are willing to sacrifice careers, relationships, family and friends, in the pursuit of authenticity. For the vast majority of us who have never questioned the appropriateness of our birth gender, it seems as though these people must be crazy or possessed. In fact, ever since the condition was first identified, theories have been spawned to explain this fascinating and rare phenomenon.

There is no definitive etiology of transsexualism. Theorists differ on whether this is an organic condition or a "conditioned condition." A long-standing psychoanalytical tradition in psychiatry has given rise to the "disorder" theory: individuals who present with gender conditions are suffering, primarily, from psychiatric disorders. Moreover, most clinicians who subscribe to this school of thought see the transsexual as having pervasive pathology. Usually they diagnose liberally from the class of disorders known as the personality disorders.

The existence of more than one disorder is called "co-morbidity." So, for instance, a transsexual may be dually diagnosed as having a gender identity disorder and a narcissistic personality disorder, or a borderline personality disorder. Recent advances in medicine and technology have caused specialists who work with gender conditions to give more weight to biological precedents.

While it is impossible to experiment on human infants, sometimes Mother Nature, in her mishaps, performs these experiments for us. Case in point: adrenogenital syndrome (AGS). In this syndrome, baby girls are born without an important enzyme which is required for the making of an adrenal hormone called cortisol. Left untreated, at four years of age they masculinize and begin to look like adolescent boys. They have mixed genitalia, which includes an oversized clitoris that resembles a penis.

Treatment for this condition became available in the 1950s. It consists of administering corticosteroids from birth on and surgically correcting the appearance of the genitals so that they are decidedly female.

With this treatment, these babies are indistinguishable from other infant girls. They are raised female and no one is aware that they are in any away different from other females. But, as these little girls mature, (and are the subject of longitudinal research studies), they all evidence behavior more typical of males than of females.

The AGS girls show a marked preference for short hair and pants, and eschew wearing dresses. They prefer competitive sports and are disinterested in dolls. They all refer to themselves as "tomboys." When they reach adulthood most don't marry; few have children. When asked directly, they say that if they could choose, they would "prefer to have been male."

The relevance of AGS is that it clearly casts doubt on the "nurture" component of the nature vs. nurture controversy. It begins to appear that transsexuals are born rather than made. An equally important construct in the theory that transsexualism is a fixed, biological condition, is the rapidly mounting assemblage of brain structure research. With sophisticated new technologies, such as functional magnetic resonance imaging and positron emission tomography, brain activity and structure can be envisaged as never before.

Brain-imaging studies reveal differences in the structure (and function) of female and male brains.

Specifically, differences have been identified in the temporal lobe, the corpus callosum, and the anterior commissure. Maybe the transsexual patients who say, "I have a female brain in a male body" are accurately describing their condition.

The old medical aphorism is true: "If you listen to your patients carefully, they will give you the diagnosis. Listen a bit longer, and they will also give you the treatment."

PLASTICS

Paula is sitting in a straight-backed chair. She is holding her left testicle in her left hand. Her face is dripping with sweat. Not one of the one hundred inhabitants of this small town know what Paula is doing inside on this sweltering day. She has persisted in her secret task, while others sit on their porch and sip lemonade.

For nearly four hours now, she has carefully separated the testicle from its sac. With her right hand she deftly uses a blade to sever the small connective blood vessels. She is not surprised by the pain or the blood, only the sluggishness of the procedure. Never did it occur to her that it would be so slow-going! Not to mention the unfortunate fact that the right testicle too, awaits removal.

Eight hours have gone by. It occurs to Paula that she may be dying. Perhaps her blade has met up with a larger blood vessel. That would account for the spreading pool beneath the chair. Quickly, she reevaluates her goals.

Yes, she wants to be free of the testosterone that is poisoning her. No, she doesn't want to die.

April 17, 1994

Eugene Schrang, M.D.
240 First Street
Neenah, WI   54956
   Re: Paula Holtz

Dear Dr. Schrang,

   I am writing to refer Paula Holtz to you for bilateral orchiectomy. Paula Holtz is a 34 year old white male to female transsexual who presented to Dr. Frederic Ettner with severe deep vein thrombosis in the iliac veins on both sides. The patient was on hormonal therapy for three months when she was admitted to the hospital with blood clots.

   The doctor who had originally prescribed feminizing hormones told her that she was no longer a candidate for hormones, and she should resign herself to living in the male gender. Dr. Ettner examined this individual, immediately consulted with me, and referred her for a complete gender evaluation.

   Paula is an extremely bright, soft-spoken individual who gives a lifelong history of gender dysphoria. At age 16, her parents confronted her about her cross-dressing. Paula was completely traumatized by their "discovery."

From that moment on, Paula vowed never to dress again, and began to pursue male activities with a vengeance. This "flight into masculinity" and the repression of authenticity proved to be disastrous for Paula: She had eight serious accidents during that time of her life, including breaking her back and cutting off part of three fingers.

After leaving home, Paula resumed her dressing, and to her amazement, found a woman who could accept this secret part of her life. Paula married her and repeatedly assured her that she did not want to change her sex, as she feared abandonment. Paula was married for three years when her wife died suddenly of a brain aneurysm.

Paula began counseling with an inexperienced therapist who encouraged Paula to put her women's clothes away and try to "normalize." The therapist spent many years trying to find psychoanalytic explanations for Paula's persistent preoccupation with changing gender.

Paula grew increasingly despondent, and in 1993 attempted to remove her own testicles. Someone discovered her self-mutilating attempt and insisted that she go to a hospital, where a surgical repair was done.

Since that time Paula has become even more despondent. Her only hope lies in finding a doctor who understands the nature of her condition and the necessity of hormonal management of some sort. Her experience *of consulting with Dr. Fred Ettner and myself was her first encounter with people who were knowledgeable about her condition. She now feels quite hopeful about the forthcoming surgical procedure and her progress towards complete sex reassignment.*

Paula is free from any thought disorders, although she is mildly depressed. She is being treated with Zoloft® and she is quite improved.

She is well-oriented and authentic looking. She understands the irrevocable nature of the surgery she is about to undergo. She is a kind, thoughtful person who is sensitive to the needs of others. I have enjoyed working with her, and helping her find some hope in life. She is financially responsible and has the money to pay for all necessary procedures.

I recommend orchiectomy for this patient. Without it her prognosis is poor, as she will lapse into despair. With the procedure completed, she will continue her gender transition and return in nine months time for completion of the genital surgery.

Sincerely, Randi Ettner

Hormonal management of the transgendered patient consists, most often, of the administration of feminizing hormones to genetic males. A typical protocol might be injections of 20 mg (1/2 cc) of estradiol one to two times per month, combined with daily doses of Premarin®. Antiandrogens, such as Spironolactone®, can be efficacious. Continuous monitoring of the patient is essential. The physical transition from male to female is dependent on time and tissue response. It cannot be hastened. Only physicians knowledgeable about the impact of hormonal therapy on every organ system should undertake management of this population.

I have been asked to speak at a seminar for plastic surgeons. The purpose of the seminar is to inform women about options in cosmetic surgery and to show slides of various procedures. My talk will be "The Psychology of Body Image." Over two hundred women are in attendance.

At lunch, I find myself seated next to a pleasant looking plastic surgeon whom I have not previously met. We are chatting, and I ask him about the nature of his practice.

"Oh," he says "breast augmentation, liposcuplting, facial peels, scar removal, tummy tucks . . . You know, all the things that make people feel better about themselves. How about you? How come a psychologist is so involved with plastic surgeons?"

"Well, I evaluate patients for sex reassignment surgery and co-manage their cases with the plastic surgeon," I say.

The gentleman hastily gets up and says "I'm leaving, rather than have an argument with you."

"What is there to argue about?" I ask, thoroughly confused.

"That," he says, "is *not* a valid surgery."

BETTER LATE THAN NEVER

It is a cold morning in April. I am seated in my office, staring at a new patient. Actually, its an old new patient. Eighty-four years old. This octogenarian has traveled to Chicago from his home in Wyoming to plead for a sex change. His story is riveting, but so is my recurring thought that he physically resembles my father, a mild-mannered accountant. We end the session and I bid him good-bye.

Almost immediately the phone rings. I'm stunned when I recognize my father's voice on the other end:

"Randi, I must speak to your about something urgent."

"Dad, please, don't tell me you need a sex change." I say, bracing myself.

"No, I'm very happy with my sex." he says, "What I need is your tax return."

Robert VanHaus was born in the Netherlands eighty-four years ago. Two years ago, he was diagnosed as having prostatic cancer. Robert had always enjoyed excellent health: swimming, walking, and playing tennis daily, weather permitting. He researched the various treatments for his illness, and found that most doctors were recommending surgical interventions. Robert inquired as to whether or not there were nonsurgical treatments for prostatic cancer. His family doctor informed him that giving estrogens to men with prostatic adenocarcinomas and metastasis was very efficacious. However, he would not be offered this protocol because doing so would greatly feminize him in the process: An unfortunate, but inevitable side effect.

Robert left his doctor's office unable to speak. He was thunderstruck. Gasping for air, he sat on a curb and tried to collect himself. Slowly, he made his way home, incanting a mantra that stripped his cocoon of denial by its poetic reverberation in his mind—"womanhood." The doctor's admonition about hormones had been a revelation. For Robert, rather than being horrified at the prospect of developing secondary female sex characteristics, was delighted! For two weeks he could think of little else. It was as if some quilter came along, in the winter of his life, to piece together the scraps and fragments, the episodes and decades, and reconfigure them into a recognizable patchwork: womanhood.

Now he understood why he preferred the company of women to men and participated in the ladies' activities at church. His identity crystallized in that defining moment: He was really a female.

In the months that followed, Robert set forth to acquire every bit of existing knowledge of men who had transformed into women. A former engineer, physicist, and researcher, he assimilated the information rapidly. Returning to his physician in his home town in Wyoming, he requested estrogen treatment. He prevailed upon his physician, insisting that not only was he aware of its feminizing effects, he welcomed them.

Robert VanHaus called my office. His accent was distinctive, his tone urgent. Three days later he sent this letter. It would be the first of many.

Dear Dr. Ettner,

The fact that you talked to me at length by phone on Thursday is deeply appreciated. What I appreciate even more is your willingness to talk to me about what completely dominates me since the end of 1992. You are not a transvestite, undoubtedly you have had contacts with numerous transvestites/transsexuals and must have a wide knowledge of the subject generally. That is the contact I so badly need.

Last year I had many letter and phone contacts with transsexuals, have read magazines and books on the subject. That has given me valuable but also at times confusing and contradictory information. It always turned out that those informants were not only transsexuals but also transvestites. I definitely am a transsexual but, equally definitely, not a transvestite. I don't desire to merely dress the part, but to be and live as a woman.

That makes me think that my condition might be rather exceptional. But you might disagree. Furthermore it seems to me that my approach to the subject might be very different from that of other transsexuals, like my way of making decisions and acting on those decisions, my way of making sure that I stay on course and don't turn round, my ability to drop habits at once, and not to mull over what might have happened if I had steered a different course. But on all those points I need your insights.

It is absolutely essential that we meet face to face. A number of facts about me you simply will not believe until you see me. A few examples. When a few years ago I lived in Greenland with an Eskimo family [we had never met before] I had to show my passport before the husband believed I was as old as I claimed to be.

Due to my exceptional vitality, energy, interest in and zest for life I often ask myself these questions: 1.) Is there a connection between the almost incredible condition of my body and mind and that at my age equally incredible, intense transsexual desire? and 2.) Could an unusual condition in my body explain these two equally incredible conditions, like for example, some female gland? Might it therefore be wise to see an endocrinologist or related specialist?

Let me now quote from the article "Transsexual Surgery" by the Los Angeles urological surgeons Julius H. Winer and Stephen D. Bloomberg which was published several years ago in **The Humanist:**

"When patients for urological sex change present themselves for their initial consultation, their opening

statements are almost routine, probably having been passed along by gossip from other applicants."

You will have noticed I did not do that. Why? Because of my integrity. That same integrity prevents me from being a transvestite. I have read somewhere, can't find it now, that many transsexuals score higher than real females when tested on female characteristics. Based on the quote above doesn't that raise the suspicion that they purposely answered the questions in a very female fashion? Here in Wyoming I answered the MMPI-2 [Minnesota Multiphasic Personality Inventory-ed.] test as honestly as I was able to and scored higher on female characteristics than on male characteristics. Why did I never think about myself in male-female terms until last year? I was simply unaware. But since the age of eleven or twelve I have been aware of acting and feeling a bit different from most males in my age group. Last year I began to realize that must be due to a large extent to strong female tendencies.

Now some practical details which might be of help to you. I am a nonsmoker, total alcohol consumption during the year is four or five glasses of wine, I only use drugs prescribed by my physician. I am NOT a homosexual, have been legally married, fathered three girls, now divorced. No criminal record, pay all my taxes. To the best of my knowledge I have a good reputation in my small home town, after fourteen years.

I don't use glasses nor a hearing aid. Every day I walk three to six miles, sun or snow. I regularly swim.

I don't mail this letter and enclosures to make myself important. I definitely am not important. It is *mailed in the hope you might have some minutes to look at it and that it will make our talks much more productive. I sure need some sound professional help badly.*

It will be a pleasure meeting you.

Sincerely, Robert

Enclosures: 1.) A Life of Change 2.) Things I need to Know 3.) What happened during 1993 4.) PSA and other test results 5.) Report on my physical condition by my present physician. 6.) Two copies of documents showing my social activities. 7.) Copies of three letters showing my professional capabilities and the one by Dr. H. testifying to my integrity. 8.) Dimensions and related characteristics of my body

I am discussing this case with my husband, a physician who does hormonal management of transsexuals, and our assistant Samantha, who is a transsexual.

"How old?" Samantha asks.

"Eighty-four," I reply.

"If you're eighty-four, and just discovering that you're a transsexual, why not just put a bow on your bald head and call yourself a woman?" Samantha asks facetiously.

I scold her, "That's called 'ageism.'"

Comorbidity is the coexistence of different diagnostic constellations in the same individual. For example, a person may be a borderline personality disorder and simultaneously be diagnosed as having an eating disorder.

Many mental health specialists unfamiliar with gender conditions are easily seduced into thinking that the gender issue is a symptom of some other primary disorder, such as schizophrenia, dissociative disorder, or one of the personality disorders such as narcissistic personality disorder. The fact that so many professionals considered transsexualism to be a symptom of schizophrenia caused many transsexuals to be misdiagnosed and inappropriately treated for psychosis.

While careful differential diagnosis must be made in each and every individual case, extensive research studies contradict the comorbidity theory. That is to say that individuals, like Robert, who present with gender conditions are no more likely than others to have comorbid conditions.

In a recently reported study from Galveston, Texas, individuals who were dually diagnosed with schizophrenia and transsexualism were evaluated. Some of the individuals in this group attained sex reassignment surgery with good outcomes. The two issues which therefore become theoretically, albeit fallaciously wedded are:

1. Is the transsexual, by definition, crazy? and,

2. Can a crazy person legitimately request surgical reassignment or is this a delusion that will lead to post-surgical regret and possible suicide?

By appointing psychologists as the gatekeepers, we tacitly agree that only the sane or at least the noneccentric need apply. As I come to know Robert, I'm burdened by the responsibility of my position. He is eccentric. He is not in the least crazy. In fact, I find him to be charming, intelligent and more fascinating than most individuals I know.

It seems so preposterous that a young woman such as myself has the "authority" to interview this extraordinary individual with a lifetime of accomplishments and proclaim him an unsuitable candidate, thereby wresting away his dream. Even a condemned criminal gets a final request granted. I proceed, feeling that Robert's urgency and thoroughness are borne of his fear of running out of time, rather than symptoms of some underlying obsessive compulsive disorder. He wants to die female. For Robert, it's an existential search for the answer to the question "Who am I really?" With no family to protect, no dependents to provide for, the ultimate reality of one's own identity comes into stark relief, stripped bare of the social overlay that envelopes most of us.

Early attempts by psychiatry to cure transsexualism failed. When Harry Benjamin (a German endocrinologist who identified the condition) published his classic work *The Transsexual Phenomenon,* the emphasis on talking patients out of their transsexualism waned. Clinicians who work in this area now focus on helping to support individuals who change gender, and assist them with the psychosocial intricacies of the transition.

They must also recommend them for hormonal treatment, and counsel them before sex reassignment surgery. Surgery cannot be performed unless the patient meets certain criteria known as the *Standards of Care.* These include one year of living in the preferred gender (the real life test) and two psychiatric letters of recommendation. One must come from a clinician who has counseled the candidate, the other must serve as an independent and confirming "second opinion".

I try to imagine Robert in lipstick, and quickly erase the image from the blackboard in my mind. All too soon though, he sends photographs which are not too far off from those I have conjured up. They differ from my imaginary ones, in that he underwent cosmetic facial surgery two months ago in his home town and appears even younger, and more feminine than when we met.

We open a file on Robert, never suspecting that we will need an entire file cabinet to contain the documents and correspondence we will accumulate in the months ahead.

The next document to arrive is a letter from Robert's physician, an internist:

To Whom It May Concern:

This is a letter of introduction to Robert VanHaus. Mr. VanHaus is a delightful very young 84 year old man. In 1984 he developed some urination difficulties and underwent transurethral prostatectomy. The tissue diagnosis was benign prostatic hypertrophy with one focus of well differentiated adenocarcinoma. This was followed conservatively. In 1992 his PSA was noted to be elevated. His prostate exam was felt to be abnormal, and he underwent needle biopsies. This revealed a moderately differentiated adenocarcinoma Gleason grade 6 involving 25% of the biopsy material from the left lobe and 100% biopsy material from the right lobe. The recurrence of this prostatic carcinoma is felt to be localized, and Mr. VanHaus has had no voiding symptoms. He continues to remain quite well and vigorous.

Mr. VanHaus had been reluctant to consider radiotherapy which had been suggested. He did, however, become interested in hormone therapy. Based in part on these medical developments, Mr. VanHaus has become increasingly interested in undergoing sex change surgery. He has expressed to me that rather than having a treatment such as orchiectomy for his prostate cancer, he would prefer to become physiologically as female as possible and to live, dress, and work as a woman. He is also aware that no treatment at all for this recurrent cancer would be a reasonable option medically.

Mr. VanHaus is an interesting and intellectual man. He also has some mild gout and hypertension which has been well controlled. His general health is excellent.

Sincerely, Dr. W.

In the weeks that follow my initial meeting with Robert he carries on an extensive, unrequited correspondence, in which he appraises me of his progress towards feminization and reiterates his desire for surgery. It is interesting to read these letters not only because of their fascinating content and extreme density, but also because they recall a different era in time. Its not often nowadays that one gets a typewritten letter, as opposed to one prepared on a word processor. Sometimes there are little handwritten notes on adorable kitty-cat stationary. I wonder if Robert VanHaus has ever even heard of e-mail. Occasionally, motivated solely by guilt, I answer:

> *Dear Robert,*
>
> *I read your most recent letter in its entirety, as well as the enclosures.*
>
> *Fondly, Randi Ettner, Ph.D.*

Individuals with gender dysphoria may spend years or decades denying their feminine feelings. When they finally acknowledge their gender conflicts, the process referred to as "discovery," they experience tremendous relief. This relief, however, is usually peppered with the anxiety of standing at the brink of the gender cliff. One can't go backward, yet crossing the gender border seems fraught with difficulty. It also takes handfuls of cash. Electrolysis, hormones, laboratory tests, counseling, legal change of documents, and maybe, surgery. If you "discover" you're a transsexual, it's best to be a very rich transsexual.

Many clinicians who encounter these individuals for the first time are struck by what they regard as obsessive components of the individual's presentation: "They are obsessed with ridding themselves of their genitals."

All too often, individuals with gender dysphoria are misdiagnosed as obsessive-compulsive personality disorders. The agitation of being "in the wrong body" gives rise to an unremitting psychic ache. Like a cosmic toothache, the pain overshadows any of life's simple pleasures. If these individuals must constantly reiterate their situation in an obsessive manner, perhaps it's because so often their explanations of how they perceive themselves fall on deaf ears.

One transsexual, living in the rural southeast, sought professional help from a succession of psychiatric caregivers. None were responsive to his pleas for help. None would consider his condition as anything other than a delusion. Finally, one psychiatrist was willing to enter into a gentlemen's agreement: "Take Anafranil® (a psychotropic drug used to treat obsessive-compulsive disorders) for three months. If after that you still persist in your desire to change your gender I will write a letter recommending you for hormones." Three months pass. The patient returns and presses the psychiatrist to uphold his end of the bargain, only to be told, that if he is still obsessing about this, he obviously is on too low a dose of Anafranil®!

Six months after his visit to Chicago, Robert VanHaus begins hormones under the management of his internist. Robert is now Roberta VanHaus. Her physician thinks she is obsessive. Roberta sends the following letter to me in which she delivers her defense to the aforementioned accusation:

Dear Dr. W.,

I know that you want to help me and for that I am deeply thankful. Because of the hormone treatment I am emotionally somewhat less stable than I have been previously. At times that must make my contacts with others a little trying. But you have shown much patience.

But to really help me, others must not have misunderstandings about my condition. But because it is unique, apparently, that can easily happen. It took me a long time before I fully understood what is going on inside me, yet you probably will agree with me that I am not particularly dumb.

When I went hurriedly through the folder you keep on my visits, I noticed that somewhere you qualified my condition as obsessive or as being an obsession. Undoubtedly my desire for a sex change has all the strength of a real obsession. But is that desire really an obsession? Not according to the Encyclopedia Americana. Let me quote:

"An obsession commonly is a thought that some kind of harm or damage is going to people or objects in the patient's environment. The thought forces itself on the individual's attention against his will and appears to him to be foreign to his sense of himself. He feels compelled, generally unsuccessfully, to fight against the thought. Although he knows intellectually that the thought is irrational and not likely to be realized he nonetheless reacts emotionally with considerable anxiety."

My desire for a sex change is almost in every aspect the opposite of what is explained above. Because I am essentially a woman I feel that desire is, in my case, perfectly natural and a real part of myself . . . I don't feel anxiety, just the opposite. The idea that during the last years of my life I will become almost identical with a woman after the menopause fills me with joy. I don't try to suppress the desire, on the contrary, all the time I am searching for ways and means to conquer the many obstacles still in my way. And those are many.

Perhaps you don't agree with me that essentially I am a female. And that is your good right. But to me it is a deep inner conviction. It has grown out of the fact that during most of my life I have occupied myself with many things which are perfectly natural for women to deal with, but are rarely performed by men, that is, in our culture.

Sincerely, Roberta

Robert is referring to a particularly painful time in his life, long, long ago. His is a life that is best characterized by change and adaptation to change. He was born in Delft, Holland, the son of a technical director of a steamship company. By the age of six, young Robert had lived in four different homes, in three different cities, and in two different countries. To deal with the heterogeneous peoples of the countries he lived in, he had to learn to speak Dutch, Indonesian, Spanish, and English. He also learned Danish later in life, and struggled to learn the very difficult language of the Eskimos, Kalaallisut, a language he still studies.

Robert has lived in villages and in large cities, at the seacoast, and in the mountains, in tropical, sub-tropical, temperate, and arctic climates. He has lived under democratic, semi-democratic and dictatorial governments. He has witnessed peaceful elections and bloody revolutions.

But the time of life Robert is recalling now, on our second visit, with a pain made more palpable due to estrogen, is 1936. The place is Buenos Aires, Argentina. Robert lived in Argentina for 23 years. He witnessed seven or eight political upheavals, finally losing track of the military coups and revolutions. He still recalls, however, his personal upheaval and the revolt of his adulterous wife, who left him for an Argentinian, a man far more "manly" than Robert. Her betrayal seems small, in the kaleidoscope of memory, compared to her abandonment of their children, and her abusiveness towards Robert. He was given custody of his three small daughters, something unheard of in a Latin culture, and raised his girls to adulthood.

It is the eve of her birthday. Roberta is turning eighty-five. She is cherishing the memory of raising her children. She has lived a good, full, and righteous life. Her conversion to womanhood is a fitting epilogue to a life of change, and adaptation to change.

There is no test, medical or psychological, to diagnose transsexualism. Very, very few transsexuals have genetic anomalies. Most have chromosomes consistent with their assigned gender and physical appearance. Likewise, there is no blood test, or hormonal workup, that can detect this condition. Therefore, as in the case of Roberta, this is primarily a self-diagnosed condition. By this it is meant that the patient must disclose his condition in order to commence treatment.

Like the patient who is told that his psychosomatic illness is "all in his head," and goes from doctor to doctor hoping to find physical evidence of his illness, Roberta expresses the hope that some physical manifestation will buttress her conviction. The conviction that she is "truly" female. Roberta refers often in her letters to her hypothesis that she possesses some vestigial female gland, or some additional x chromosome.

Working with Dr. Mark Schacht, urologist, at the National Center for Advanced Medical Education, we made the following clinical observation: Males who present to my clinic as transsexuals appear, on average, to be taller than normal men. Studying one hundred patients who attained sex reassignment surgery, we set out to document this observation. The results are statistically significant. Transsexuals are taller, on average, than normal males.

The implications of this finding are substantial. It is known that testosterone in males closes the growth plates in the long bones. Therefore, the fact that these individuals are taller may indicate an insensitivity in the receptor sites to testosterone. This could very well be a genetic process and one that mandates further research, particularly tissue examination. A similar study reported findings that transsexuals are three times as likely to be left-handed as other individuals. These studies lend support to possible physiological antecedents of the condition. Roberta may yet be vindicated.

To date, Roberta remains anxious to proceed to surgical sex reassignment. She has not been successful in finding a surgeon willing to perform the operation on her. She is currently contacting surgeons in Europe.

CLOTHES DON'T MAKE
THE MAN

Marty has been dressing like a man all his life. In fact, it took tremendous, repetitive pressure from both parents, to try to persuade him, at age three, that he wasn't a boy. They failed. He was downright insistent. His parents were equally insistent that "little Mary act like a little lady."

Oddly enough, Marty wasn't confused by this gender jousting. He knew who he was, and if they couldn't see it, well then they were blind. At first, his parents were likely to regard it as stubbornness. But it went far beyond that. It was a petrification of identity that was absolutely impenetrable. If this child were not gender dysphoric, this very same trait—this determination and conviction— would be regaled as a virtue by the parents. They would proudly talk about how spunky and confident their child was. But in fact, they were horrified. Would this "tomboy" girl grow up to be a lesbian? Or worse, end up in

some loony bin where *everyone* thinks they are someone they are *not*. After all, what's the difference between
some fruitcake who thinks that he's Napoleon, and a girl
who insists she's a guy?

It was more than these apprehensions that tore the
parents' marriage apart. But the stress and the shame
were two of the straws that "broke the camel's back." It
was downright *embarrassing* to have this girl child running around naked, pretending that various elongated
objects were her "missing penis." For the child, the
father's departure was a relief. The mother was too pre-
occupied with her own crumbling life to pay much
attention to stick and pencil penises.

The years flew by, and Marty sank into resignation.
He feared he would always be regarded as a tomboy—a
term he despised. He perceived himself to be a *real* man,
not just a girl who liked to "climb trees."

The army was a temporary solution. There, Marty
was able to exercise his "aggressiveness," and strength
in an acceptable way. He flew transport jets during Desert
Storm. He was too different from the other women in the
armed forces to enjoy the intimacy and sustenance of
friendship, but at least he was tolerated.

The women in his unit found him curious. He was a
little bull dog of a person. They did not suspect him of
being a lesbian—they knew lesbians. They were certainly
uneasy being in "close quarters" with him. There was
some degree of flirtatiousness in the way he seemed to
"admire" them. They felt an undeniable and indescribable discomfort in the presence of this supposed peer. If
only they knew! Marty, who looked to all the world like
a female, was really a man in their midst! His inner

maleness seemed to invisibly seep out through his very pores and repel the women in the barracks.

Marty knew nothing whatsoever about gender dysphoria. He never heard the word transsexual. He knew though, that he was different than any other living person he had ever come across. The worst part—the very, very worst part—was the blood that came monthly, without fail. That was what he hated most.

The women in the army laughingly referred to their monthly menses as "the curse." Marty saw himself to be truly cursed and the blood was the symbol of his bane. He despised his body . Once, after leaving the army, he happened to experiment with a breast binding that pleased him. He was able to wrap the breasts in such a way as to make them unnoticeable. Of course, he was never without a shirt, and although he loved the water and the Lake of the Ozarks, he had not gone swimming, since the age of seven.

Moving anonymously through a rural life, Marty would claim to be a man and was never questioned. In fact, when he went to the department of motor vehicles to get a driver's license he gave his preferred name, Marty. With his gruff demeanor, they automatically assumed him to be male, and duly noted "M" on the document. Had they scrutinized this person closely, they would have puzzled at the lack of an "Adam's Apple," and the absence of any facial hair on the beautifully smooth face. But no one suspected and Marty continued with his "gender transition," although he never would have described it as such.

Not surprisingly, Marty lived an isolated life. Occasionally, he was able to pick up a girl in a bar and have "sex" with her. No women ever saw him naked, and the sex consisted mostly of kissing and fondling women. It was immensely satisfying, though for many reasons, not the least of which was the confirmation that he was able to pass as a man. When Marty was twenty-one, he met a woman he was genuinely fond of. Susie was a shy, hard-working girl, who ran her dad's souvenir store in the Ozarks. She married the "strange little man." That was four years ago and, to this day, her parents can't understand why Susie doesn't seem able to have babies.

It was pure happenstance that Susie was home with a cold one morning and took a look at the newspaper. She came upon an article about a doctor in another state who performed an operation on men who wanted to become women. "Maybe that same doctor could fix Marty," she thought.

That night, right after supper, Susie told Marty about the doctor. Marty was astonished. He didn't know which was more amazing: the idea that there were enough people who wanted to change their gender that a doctor could make a living at it, or that there were men who wanted to be females. Marty couldn't understand why someone who was lucky enough to be born a real guy would want to "go and cut it off."

The very next morning, Marty placed a long distance phone call to the doctor who was mentioned in the article. He didn't even know how to ask the question he wanted answered. Luckily, the receptionist intuited the question, almost before he had quite finished formulating it. She was quite accustomed to responding to people like Marty. She patiently gave him the information that would change his life.

It's a long drive from the Ozarks to Chicago. Marty doesn't mind. He usually takes an extra day to visit his mother, who is living in Wisconsin. Injections of testosterone have transformed Marty, physically and emotionally. He and Susan are delighted. Marty has an auburn beard and powerful pectoral muscles. Mastectomy has obviated the need to bind his breasts, and he proudly goes out-of-doors without a shirt as soon as the warm weather comes to Missouri. He's not self-conscious about the scars below his nipples; he's too proud of the sprouting chest hair to mind that.

Everyone in the world thinks Marty is a man. Everyone that is, except for the woman I am talking to on the phone right now. Actually she has me on hold. I use this interval to collect my thoughts about the inevitable discourse that we are about to engage in, with Marty's full permission. She is going to tell me that Marty is Mary, a woman. I am going to tell her that Marty is Marty, a man. Only one of us will be victorious in this battle. When the bell rings, we both come out swinging.

"Good afternoon Ma'am. I'm with the Bureau of Vital Statistics." Her sweet, Southern accent belies the pugnacity of her intentions. She is out to kill a man I have grown quite fond of.

"Good afternoon. How can I help you?" I can help her by telling her to take her bureaucratic documents and shove them, I think to myself.

"I'm calling about an individual who is trying to change a birth certificate. Has this individual had sexual reassignment?" she asks pleasantly.

"Yes." I reply, politely. I'm loaded for bear.

"Can you describe the nature of the reassignment?" she asks.

"Pick, pick, pick," I think to myself. "She's a sly one."

"This patient has been hormonally reassigned," I say matter of factly, gearing up for the next skirmish.

"What about surgical reassignment?" she asks.

"Yes," I respond , "the patient has had surgery." This is no lie, as the patient has had total bilateral mastectomy. Maybe, I'll wear her down and she'll tire of this verbal tug-of-war.

"Can you describe the nature of the surgery?" she asks, nonplused.

With a sinking heart I tell her.

"But what about the genital surgery?" she demands. All is lost. Without a penis, she condemns him to remaining female on microfiche, for eternity.

The surgical construction of a penis is a medical and technological wonder. Often, it is formed from skin taken from the forearm. It is a laborious and imperfect procedure, and it is extremely expensive. Cosmetically, the outcome is quite acceptable. Few female-to-male transsexuals opt for phalloplasty, the technical name for this procedure for the obvious reasons. Most choose, as does Marty, to live as men, without genital confirmation surgery. They must always face the uncomfortable situation of using the stall in the men's bathroom, rather than standing to urinate.

The world is as fascinated by this procedure as they are by the surgery that separates Siamese twins. Intrigued by the unusual, drawn to the bizarre, they clamor for details about sex reassignment surgery. Often, when people learn that someone has had such surgery, they are interested in little other than the particulars of the procedure. How do they create the penis, everyone wants to know. At times this curiosity is legitimate, and it is useful to educate people about such procedures and how successful they are.

At other times the voyeurism of the onlookers is cruel and derisive. Sometimes, I think that the transsexual is the only person that is still politically correct to scorn. We trot them out and parade them on television, and ask an "expert" to explain their freakishness.

On one occasion, I confess to having lost my patience with a mean-spirited heckler.

"So how do they make the balls?" he asks, laughing uproariously.

"With matzo meal and water," I say glibly.

*The author, a female-to-male adolescent,
and his mother*

Debbie, a physician, before and after transition

Gary, before becoming Glenda

Linda and Glenda, a married couple

Robert

Roberta

Tom

Terri

Carl

Carla

Thomas

Samantha, my assistant

KENTUCKY
Genuine Risk

It is Spring in Louisville. I have heard that Kentucky is pretty; thoroughbred horses, blue grass, and a river that runs through the city. The gift shop at the airport suggests that many visitors leave this state having been witness to these joys of nature, or to Kentucky's big attraction, the Derby.

The Kentucky I know is not pretty at all. It is a Holiday Inn off an interstate, as tacky as they come. It is here that I will hole up for the next twenty-four hours while a strange parade of life's casualties file past me, one by one, every 55 minutes.

I have no one to blame for it but myself. I had an idea one day which has led me to this tacky Holidome. This Holidome, in particular, because a person who looks strange, and doesn't want to be seen in public can sneak up to my room without having to go through the lobby.

A person who is neither (according to society) man or woman, can park a pickup in the lot out back, and head up a dark stairway to a genderless sanctuary.

It began one year ago when I brought in the mail. There was a pamphlet addressed to me from a member of Harvard University's Department of Psychology. It was a manual on how to treat people who had been abducted by aliens. Aliens! It started with a warning that it's quite likely that a counselor would see an "abductee" at one point in their professional career and should be knowledgeable as to how to treat these people. I must confess I didn't read the whole pamphlet because I'm afraid of people from other planets, and it gave me the jitters. But then I came upon an idea. If they can educate me about aliens, why can't *I* educate them about transsexuals, whom they treat like aliens for the most part, anyway. So I thought about Kentucky, because in that whole state, not one professional who is knowledgeable about gender has ever come forth to assist people with gender conditions.

So, I informed a group of patients who had been driving seven hours each way to see me in Chicago, that I would come to Kentucky. I told the support group there to tell all the mental health professionals that they've ever worked with, and all the health care providers, that I will come to Kentucky and offer them free training and supervision, and educate them about working with the transgendered. We reserved a large auditorium at a local university and received lots of publicity. My publicist in New York had even arranged for television coverage.

"I think it would make great footage if you and Abby (a transsexual patient) are filmed shopping together here in Louisville."

"Shopping!" I sputter. I'm incredulous that my publicist would stoop so low. "No, no, no. That is totally nonprofessional. Since when do psychologists go shopping with their patients?" I bark.

Now, some three hours later, Abby and I are sitting across a large auditorium, vacant, save for the two of us. Not one person accepted my offer. Not one person showed up.

"Now what?" I ask.

"Want to go shopping?" suggests Abby.

"Sure," I reply. "Let's hit the mall!"

We are speeding down a highway, Abby and I, both of us buried in thought. Abby breaks her reverie to share with me a dream she has had since childhood. As soon as she starts to relate it, I mentally wander off. It is The Dream, the one I hear all the time. The one in which the boy child goes to bed and awakens as a girl.

"Did I ever tell you about this dream I had as a kid?" she asks.

"I don't think so."

"Well, I go to bed and the next..."

By now I am mentally halfway through my lecture notes. In my mind's theater I am playing to a packed audience. I am educating the entire state of Kentucky on the misunderstood subject of gender dysphoria— people who are uncomfortable with their genetic, assigned gender.

"What is the role of the psychologist in working with the gender dysphoric patient?" I ask this imaginary group of caregivers. I scan the audience for signs of intelligence, and seeing none in their imaginary faces I plunge ahead:

"First and foremost it is to educate the individual about this condition. I believe this condition is neuroanatomical. The condition is not curable. It requires multi-disciplinary management by psychologists, endocrinologists, and often surgeons.

The psychologist must help the patient work through the guilt and shame that is always a part of this condition. Help the person to understand that they must acknowledge this condition. They have choices about how to live in this world with this condition. Maybe if this were a better world, this wouldn't be such a bad condition. Support the person through the difficult time of transition to the desired gender. Educate employers and human resource people about the necessity of various surgical procedures. Help them to attain documents that support their chosen gender. Provide support, education, and counseling for the families and significant others. Provide postsurgical support for the individual who chooses sex reassignment surgery. Life is an ongoing process that neither begins nor ends with gender reassignment."

Abby parks the pickup and turns off the engine.

"Abby, that is a powerful dream," I say, waking from mine.

"Finally, for me it's reality," she says, beaming.

Abby is my friend. I was the last professional to see her before she went under the knife. I gave her the go-ahead so that a surgeon would alter her body and allow it to conform to her identity and psyche. Abby used to be Edward. I did not know him. I knew he was a miserable human being, though. Taunted and humiliated throughout his childhood, he was always accused of being gay, or worse, he was simply ignored. As an adult he joined the army but spent his weekends driving around dressed in women's clothing. Edward married three times, each disastrously, then hit rock bottom. Then came the awakening, followed by therapy, hormones, and transition. Abby emerged. She went to school, had sex reassignment surgery, and is living a productive life.

As we walk through the mall, I have the feeling that everyone is staring at us. In truth, everyone *is* staring. We are an odd-looking pair. I am 5'1" and dressed in my best business suit. Abby is 6'1" and wearing the shortest shorts imaginable. Her legs are long and thin, definitely her best feature. It helps that her male genetic material is not programmed, like mine, to seduce cellulite and entrap it to the thighs. She wears big, blond wig-hair, and lots of jewelry. Ostensibly, we have nothing in common. Abby's hobby is propositioning truckers she picks up on her CB. My hobby is reading. Our friendship is simple. The thin wire that connects us is gender. I understand Abby; that's why she likes me. I like her because she has a heart as big as the Holidome.

Every suite at the Holiday Inn Holidome in Louisville is named after a Derby winner. My suite is Genuine Risk. This is the first auspicious thing that has occurred since

I came to Kentucky. As if this place weren't bad enough, they threatened to put me in the Swale Suite. Swale won the Derby in 1984, but died soon after.

For several months, a small band of gender people have been "putting back" money for a consultation with me. Today is the day they have been waiting for. Here, in this dingy room, they will take the genuine risk of revealing to a complete stranger a dangerous secret: they long to live in a different body. Life in this gender is a mistake. The brain and body are at constant war and the soul is dying.

It takes me several minutes to compose myself. I am not prepared for the poverty of these people. I am not prepared for the reverence with which they treat me. They are awed by the spaciousness of my rented suite. I am appalled by the megadoses of hormones they are taking. I take the genuine risk of practicing medicine without a license and give them prescribing information about hormones. Then there are the stories! Each one is so full of pain and pathos, that by lunch I feel broken.

Twenty-four hours later, I am leaving Kentucky. On my way through the airport I stop at the gift shop and pick up a state magnet for my kids. I need no souvenirs. I am taking home stories that I will never forget. One in particular haunts me. It rattles in my head on the airplane and I feel compelled to write it down. It is a lasting reminder that truth is stranger than fiction.

Rochelle's Story

Rochelle is a fat, forty-ish woman who is seated across my hotel room. She looks like she has been poured into the clothes she wears, like a sausage coming out of its casing. Her hair is long and disheveled. Folks around here probably refer to her as poor white trash. But if they were to peek in her underwear, they would really be surprised! Poor white transsexual trash.

Twenty years ago Rochelle was pretty. Pretty and passable. In fact, we clinicians call her a primary transsexual. She never even tried to live as a man. Twenty years ago, pretty young Rochelle went to a party. She had too much Kentucky moonshine and eyed a gorgeous man across the room. He returned her glance and sparks flew.

Soon the young couple found themselves in bed. In the throes of passion, Rochelle's anatomical secret became highly visible: she had a penis. How shocking to the lover! However, Rochelle was in for a surprise herself. This charming young man was a female! Yes, "he" had a vagina. He was a female-to-male transsexual!

That night a child was conceived. Conceived and born by a genetic female who wanted, more than anything in the world, to lose every vestige of womanhood. The baby was put up for adoption.

Rochelle was in a state of agitation that bordered on mania. The child was hers—she was the "mother." She felt a love for the baby girl that would leave a hole in her heart forever. Rochelle went to court in the vain attempt to get custody of her daughter. The judge said she was a sick, disturbed human being who should never be allowed near the child. The child was given to a couple for adoption.

Late that night, Rochelle sneaked into a hospital somewhere in rural Kentucky. When she left, she took a tiny baby in a shoe box home with her. She loved and nurtured that newborn for three days and three nights.

Then her mama caught sight of the baby girl. Her mama saw right away that the baby girl was black. Her mama called the police and they took away Rochelle's baby.

ZOMBIES

It's a Halloween straight out of a Stephen King novel. The wind is blowing sheets of rain against my bedroom window. Me—in bed with pneumonia and a basket of Halloween candy. Can't foretell if I will die tonight or just gain several pounds and live on as a short, fat, stumpy woman with permanently weakened lungs.

A rain-drenched three-foot lion appears at my door:

"Mommy, can you take me trick-or-treating?"

The child does not realize I can eat but can't breathe. "Sorry, babe. I'm too sick."

A neighbor miraculously arrives in a floor-length poncho and whisks the lion out into the blustery night rain. Later I will learn that his costume and his ego were dampened, when he is mistaken for a sunflower.

Not one trick or treater. I was hoping to banish the boredom of bed rest with a tiny parade of ghosts and witches. Alone, and racked with pain, I try to catch up on my reading. I turn to a seminal work on transvestites, translated from the German, but my mind wanders. I phone a friend.

"Barbara, can you drive the kids to school tomorrow?"

"Sure. Still sick, huh?"

"Barbara. I'm dying. Can I give you the phone numbers of all my old boyfriends? Notify them if I pass on and ask them to think of me when I was thin and youthful."

"Can I do it now? I may be too busy later. Besides, what's the point? You'll continue to hound them, even after you're dead. You're insufferable. You'll haunt us all forever."

Once, in Houston, I saw a zombie. For real.

It was August of 1994, and I was invited to speak at the TransGen Conference. This is a yearly symposium, chaired by attorneys, and dedicated to disseminating information about the legal rights of transsexuals. It has been described as a "transsexual think tank." It is held in Houston and has a decidedly radical flavor. These people are in your face.

I'm surprised to learn that Dr. Eugene Schrang, a sex reassignment surgeon, and myself are the only professional caregivers invited to speak. For three days, individuals with gender conditions can choose to attend workshops on documents, employment or health issues. In the evenings, there are meetings about organizing to change legislation and make political headway on the local levels. There is valuable firsthand advice about how to transition on the job and remain employed.

Day one

I arrive and am immediately politically incorrect. Seems I have displayed brochures which contain the phrase "gender dysphoria." Apparently, this is a no-no. A large, mean-looking transsexual snarls at me and informs me: "That term is a psychiatric diagnosis and we won't tolerate that." She looks like she wants to bite my leg. She was probably a very sweet, lovely person before coming here, I tell myself. Houston in August is so hot and humid that anyone could go on a psychotic rampage. I'm beginning to wonder what I'm doing here.

Day two

Better. I have redeemed myself by giving a stirring presentation on the psychologists' role in gender conditions. I am no longer the enemy. In fact, I have been introduced as the "caregiver of the 90s." Even yesterday's transsie from hell is genial. I am answering questions, buoyed by an excess of caffeine, when I see a figure approach. I break off mid-sentence. I am watching a man approach me who is not man at all. There is something eerie and nonhuman about his demeanor. I stare, transfixed by his appearance. I am staring at a zombie.

Perhaps it is the eyes. They are the biggest, bluest eyes I have ever seen. As we sit, the eyes meet mine with such tenacity that I have trouble concentrating on the words. The words are like a song, but I can't hear the music and lyrics simultaneously. I am too distracted by the eyes. This must be what attention deficit disorder is like.

The zombie tells me that he has lost thirty pounds in thirty days. That is why the eyes are so piercing! I realize that the skin hangs on this person like a size 6x would on a newborn. An emaciated blue-eyed skeleton. Like someone liposuctioned my daughter's cabbage patch doll, leaving only some wire limbs and pasted-on blue eyes.

The zombie is a lawyer. Was a lawyer. Now he is a goner, as far as I can tell. Still he intimidates me like a trial lawyer at a deposition arguing my credentials. "Stop these thoughts!" I shout to myself. "Pay attention! You are audience to a personal tale of horror and you are losing details like water through a sieve." Try as I might, all I remember of the story is the "bare bones." It goes like this:

I was Harry Benjamin's patient. The famous German endocrinologist who identified transsexualism—the father of trannsexualism. He treated all of the transsexuals, even Christine Jorgensen. I was an early patient of his, some thirty years ago. He and a psychiatrist approved me for surgery.

It was rather experimental then, and they sent me to Mexico for sex reassignment. I was operated on and mutilated, really. I woke up from the anesthesia, screaming. They helicoptered me to San Francisco. A plastic surgeon there did an emergency repair. Really, an amputation that left me without genitals—genderless.

I returned out East to my parents, living as the female I always believed myself to be. I went to Johns Hopkins, to the best psychiatrist. You know who I'm talking about. He treats me with psychoanalysis and tells me I can't be female because I am too much con-sumed with motorcycles. I must revert to living as a man. He "assigns" me a gender.

I flee the East and find a psychiatrist in the Bay Area who claims to be knowledgeable. He puts me on massive doses of testosterone to masculinize me. "No sense changing gender. You will never have an authentic female anatomy. Live as a man."

The testosterone is poisoning me. Still, even with the testosterone, I never lose it . . . the feeling that I am female. I heard you today, and think about what your profession has done to me, and felt that you should know. I am phoning my doctor now. Telling him no more male hormones. Female hormones . . . estrogen. Tell me what's the proper dosage?"

Day three

A tall emaciated woman with gigantic blue eyes wanders through the crowd. It is the zombie, in an ill-fitting wig and dress. She has begun her gender transition. Again.

I phone my husband and describe the zombie. He has a perfectly logical explanation: "Giving massive amounts of testosterone to a castrated male may have created a condition of anabolism and a shutdown of the pituitary gland, possibly the adrenals. That accounts for his bizarre zombie-like appearance. He probably can't assimilate nutrients or salts."

We discuss the kids and then he returns to the zombie: "Imagine three decades of oscillating between genders. His body is a battleground where the medical sovereigns play out their opposing views . . . Is this a legitimate disorder, or is it not? After thirty years the debate continues."

It is evening now and the Southwest Hilton is empty. The conference participants have headed out for dinner and a night on the town. Me—alone, drained and hungry. In the hotel lobby I plop down in front of a kindly concierge who is as wide as the desk that divides us. We discuss the pros and cons of various Mexican restaurants, and I choose, judiciously. She arranges my transportation. Suddenly a man appears. Out of nowhere. A traveler. A genetic male.

"Will you be my guest for dinner?" he asks, innocently.

"No." I say, bitchily. "I'm a happily married woman."

He looks stung by my rebuff. To his credit, he rallies. "I'm married with four children," he offers.

I glance at the concierge who watches this transaction. She beams like a rabbi blessing this ersatz union. The man and I leave together.

Charming man and bottled beer have me intoxicated. I forget the zombie. The man seems to have forgotten some demons of his own. I need a moment of anonymous intimacy to retrieve my soul, but this moment lasts for hours. Some non-ordinary reality of vulnerability, chemistry, and conversation is overtaking me.

I feel like Alice in Genderland, with a Corona that says "Drink me." If I don't back away now, I might fall into a hole that I can't get out of. So I quickly return to Chicago, where cold autumn realities blow away the malaise and the man.

It's Halloween. The past month has been business as usual. There were many new patients and a suicide. I have all but forgotten the zombie. His story is like a book I read and returned to the library. There have been many more stories since. Sometimes, I still think about the man.

THE SELF
A House Divided

Few people are aware that there is an inner self and an outer self. For most people, the two fuse to create a homogeneous self-system. That is to say, that most people look in the mirror and recognize who they see as the "me." There is no incongruity between the perceived self and the reflected self. For certain individuals, the outer self may be a distortion or exaggeration of the "me." So the obese individual, for example, often expresses the belief that there exists a thin person inside. But this notwithstanding, the belief is that the real self is a "pared down" version of the visible self; but the concept of "self" is still integral.

For the transsexual, there is a clear dichotomy between the inner and outer self. They are in no way interchangeable, or even complementary. Indeed, the outer self and the inner self are diametrical. The outer self is like a "shell" that belies the very existence of an inner, counter self. The fundamental plight of transsexuals is that the world relates and responds to them as though they are the shell. This creates a continuous internal ecology of forever *feeling* misunderstood and having to act uncharacteristically, to meet society's expectations.

The following materials introduce a transsexual patient named Kristin. Here, in her own words, she speaks to the feelings of having an outer self that has failed the inner. The incongruity of her condition results in her own personal transition. The anguish, the acceptance, and ultimately the determination to rectify her situation, was expressed through journal entries and our correspondence. The decision to make this life-change was not an easy one—one that she would have to justify not only to herself, but to many in society as well.

February 24, 1994

Dear Dr. Ettner,

I promised to send you something before my consultation with you. I apologize in advance for the length of this piece. I prepared this a while ago from different bits and pieces for a transsexual person I was in correspondence with in Gibralter (of all places). A number of people have found it helpful, and as I sat down to edit it, I kept running out of steam and time. Probably anything you want is in the first section entitled December 1992.

*Looking forward to seeing you at 10 AM
on March 18.*

Sincerely, Dr. Kristin Rachael

This is the story of a long journey to today, and hopefully, to far beyond.

December 1992

My ancient history has elements of many such stories: I suffered physical abuse over an extended period when young, had an emotionally distant father, became aware at the age of four of wanting to be a girl, experimented with my sister's clothes, felt joy then guilt, felt confusion as puberty came along and I was attracted to girls both because I loved them and because I wanted to be them, attempted suicide at sixteen, had intensive counseling to "cure" me of wanting to be a woman.

After college I married a "wonderful" woman who at first said my cross dressing didn't matter and then had trouble dealing with it, was divorced after fifteen years of marriage (no children to complicate the issue), entered immediately into another relationship with a woman, probably believing that she could "save" me from my wanting to be a woman, then moved from the big city to a rural state when that relationship ended, quickly fell in love with another woman, hoping to live a "normal" life, to be saved, only to have that relationship fail when she realized she couldn't deal with the cross dressing. I then had a one-month relationship with a woman who had been a good friend until then. Somehow that got screwed up.

Now we are up to early August. I am forty-five years old, have a decent job, a wonderful house in a picturesque location, but my subconscious is screaming "Now is the time; now go for what you want; become the woman you are."

But my conscious mind wouldn't listen. I can't sleep, I start to drink too much, and I start to think thoughts of suicide. However, my conscious mind doesn't know why I am feeling so depressed. Oh, sure, it knows that I want to be a woman, but it knows all the reasons why that can't happen.

My therapist tries to help me, and she asks me why I wouldn't go ahead with what I want. So I rehearse for her the reasons I have been using for years: I am too old (wouldn't we all wish to be young women if we could be—with years of experiences ahead of us?), I have a comfortable life that would be shattered if I went ahead with this. I would probably lose my job and my house, and the latter would really hurt, because for the first time, I feel I am "home." I have too much body hair and it would take years of electrolysis to have it removed, and on and on and on.

So summer stretches into fall, and my depression deepens to the point that every weekend I visit a different location in this rural state and decide how I will commit suicide. I even make a list of the places I find and the advantage and disadvantage of each.

But while all this is going on, my subconscious is fighting to be heard. In May, it located an illegal source of hormones, and I started taking them, believing in the evidence in the literature that very low dosages of hormones can deter potential transsexuals from becoming "full blown" transsexuals. And in July, I started to collect information from those on T* (transvestite, transgendered, transsexual) bulletin boards about their hormone usage for an FAQ (frequently asked questions); and I spent nearly every lunch time in the library reading T* books and articles I had read years ago. My conscious mind was denying the obvious purpose of all this, and my subconscious mind was doing all it could to be heard—and thus the two were like two trains steaming towards each other on the same track. I was a crisis waiting to happen.

Finally it did; in November I attempted suicide again, but, as we know, many suicides are simply calls for help, and thus are often done in such a way that they will not succeed. So in my case—I lived through my attempt—but my subconscious got its way, the suicide got the voice of the subconscious heard.

More intensive counseling, and then, in the middle of the night near Thanksgiving, I had the worst anxiety attack of my life. I thought my heart would explode; I was covered with sweat, but I couldn't figure out what I was so anxious about. Of course, it just so happened that I had counseling the next day, but in the middle of the night, I didn't put two and two together. (Of course, my subconscious mind had.)

At the session that day, my therapist and I talked about the anxiety attack, about my continuing thoughts of suicide, and she asked me again to list the reasons why I didn't want to go ahead and live as a woman. As I listed each reason, it was like the sun burst through the window: the whole room became brighter and I could "see" my future; each reason seemed silly in comparison to the happiness I now felt in consciously embracing the possibility of sex reassignment surgery (SRS). She could see in my face my decision, and simply said "It has been a long road, hasn't it?"

That night I called my sister and told her of my decision to become a woman. It was a great call; she challenged me to explain my needs and reasons and helped me to think through the issues even better. Over the next week, I told the rest of the female members of my family (found it hard to tell my brothers), I legally went on hormones and spironolactone, started electrolysis, and told a dozen of my friends and co-workers. Several said they weren't surprised, none seemed to have a problem with it. (Thank goodness many of us in this state take a private approach to religion, so I have no fundamentalists to worry about). Some of those people told their children, who, by and large, seem to have taken it better and accepted it more quickly.

The euphoria wore off, and I have begun to make plans for "transitioning," wondering how they will take it at work, but not particularly caring. I am going to take the hard road—do it here, in full view of society, ala Renee Richards, trying to keep my job and friends instead of moving to a new city and beginning there where people don't know me. Oh sure, I know the difficulties of this approach—at the very least 90 percent of the people I come into contact with at work shall know of my biological past—and, working in a University as I do, the students shall pass that on to each new generation of students. Outside the University it is a small, rural world, and they will know—but it is also a community that leaves people alone.

Depression set in when I realized how little help there is for me in this part of America. There are no gender clinics, few other transsexuals, and so no one to turn to for advice, support, or a shoulder to lean on. There is no easy way to get advice on SRS, to hear stories of making the transition, etc.

I knew I would survive. After all, I have until now as a man; I just need to hold on a little longer until I can be*come* the woman I guess I would have wished to marry—a strong, independent woman who does her job well, has a few close friends, and cares about them.

Winter 1993

In January I fell into a really deep depression; I missed suicide only because the logging truck that was coming towards me (I was in his lane) swerved at the last moment. I realized a few days later that I was so depressed because of a failure I was having in contacting pre- and post-op transsexuals to get advice and to talk about their experiences. In this rural state, there is no support available of any type, and I hoped that I would be able to get such via e-mail. Many post-ops failed to respond, and the advice from pre-ops greatly varied. Some said don't transition on the job—leave the city, state, etc; others said stay on the job and don't run.

My depression resulted, I realized, because I was waiting for someone to give me a road map of how to get from X to the RLT (Real Life Test) and beyond. I wanted a text book. I pulled out of the depression when I realized there is no text book because there is no right and wrong here. Each of us comes to this point from many different places and with different baggage. And each of us has to walk the road that is correct for her. February went well; I slowly started to tell trusted friends.

And I suppose the inevitable happened—I received some strong challenges to my plans (all well-meaning of course). Two examples follow.

Dear Dr. Rachael,

As a biologically-determined female living within my female gender I have developed a feminist outlook because of the way society views women. I would like to know how you, as a biologically-determined male proposing to live within a female gender, will feel. I find it frustrating knowing that women are second-class citizens, socially, economically, even spiritually. We receive less for our efforts, fewer rewards for them, and little credit for our inner strengths (which aren't always "feminine ones"). Many women suffer. A few succeed. Most of us cope.

In this world where so much blame, hatred and mistrust is meted out to women, how can you, born a man with all the "advantages" society gives you, be so willing to give all that up to live as a woman? I perceive in you, in what I have heard second or third hand, a strong desire for the accouterments of a feminine ideal—the clothes, the hair, the very feminine name—but I really want to know if you are willing to understand and put up with all that it takes to be a female in a man's world.

I responded in part:

You ask if I am "willing to understand and put up with what it takes to be a female in a man's world." This is a very fair question, but I think you will agree that I can answer that question honestly only when I have, indeed, lived as a woman for some period of time. Otherwise I would simply be paying lip service to my supposedly liberal nature. Oh, it is true that, over the years, I have witnessed much of what you describe regarding the way in which society treats, or more appropriately, mistreats women.

However, I cannot pretend that I will ever truly know the full degree of the "blame, hatred and mistrust . . . meted out to women." Certainly, I shall experience some of that, but most of the negative reaction I shall receive will come from the fact that nearly all around me know that I am neither male nor female but transsexual. At the worst, in the minds of some, I will be seen as a freak of nature and something to be despised. In the minds of others, I shall be viewed as a threat or challenge to their own conceptions of gender and behavior.

You also ask "how I can be so willing to give up (all the advantages society gives men) to live as a woman." Again, a very fair question, and I will have to admit that I am cheating in this respect. I am not, like many other transsexuals, abandoning my current life, my friends, my job, and my home to start over in a city where no one knows of me, taking on a job and salary that society may choose for me because I am perceived *to be female. On July 6, I will bring with me into my new life the achievements that I have accrued in 46 years as a male.*

If I had been born a woman, I am certain that would have stood in the way of some of my achievements. For example, I can well imagine that such attitudes would have made it difficult for me to earn a Ph.D. from the University of Chicago in only three years while being married (as I was); they would have made it difficult for me to hold the succession of jobs that I have; they would have made it difficult for me to be chosen for this job.

But, of course, the true question is not where I have come from as a man, but were I shall go from here. And the irony is that I fully realize my career progression is probably over. Were I a genetic woman and had the achievements above, I undoubtedly could go on to a much better job from here; as a transsexual, however, I shall be able to go no further up the ladder. I shall be a victim of the "blame, hatred and mistrust meted out to transsexuals." So how shall I do in this new life? From extensive communication with others, I know that many who have made this journey before me have suffered, a few have chosen to end their life, some have coped, and very, very few have succeeded. But this is the row I have chosen to hoe.

Finally, in some minds there may be a question as to whether in the future I shall presume to make judgments about the experiences of women and whether I shall presume to speak for them as if I did, indeed, understand the full nature of their suffering. To do so would be an act of extreme hubris. No, the life I shall live will be that of a sexual bastard, the illegitimate offspring of the male and female genders, metaphorically carrying something of each gender without having the right to claim my place in either.

But I shall survive.

Why am I "so willing to give up all the 'advantages' that society gives men . . . to live as a "transsexual?"

I don't know; I simply know I must.

Following is my response to a more spirited challenge from another:

Dear X,

I read your letter, it appears a major concern of yours is whether, by choosing this course of action, I am to miss out on certain experiences/opportunities that I could only have as a male. Yes, certainly, that is true. But does that matter? To live is to make choices, and each of these choices opens as many doors as it closes. Over a decade ago, I had a vasectomy. Would you have written me the same letter suggesting I not have a vasectomy because I would never know the joy of being a parent? And would you have argued, as you do in essence later in your letter, that having a vasectomy would be to argue with "God," since I denied a possibility (having a child) that "God" gave me?

You ask, quoting the EST training, "Can you afford the arrogance that no such thing exists, the knowing of which, your life would be transformed?" And later you write, "Our gender is like a little block of granite that God assigns to us, it is where we place our feet in the Universe, and it is hubris, the most frightful hubris, to argue with God on this matter." I would like to address these together, because I believe they are the same question.

You ask whether I have the arrogance, the hubris, to question the hand dealt to me by life—whether I have the arrogance, the hubris, to refuse to accept the decision of God in the gender assigned to me. I believe you know I do not believe in a god which directs or even cares about the lives of individuals, but, accepting your appeal to God as a metaphor for the natural and biological patterns into which we find ourselves placed, I must remind you that the history of humankind, and the lessons of much of the Bible tell us that our lives are a trial and that we must, in our own ways, confront the burdens placed before us. The trials of Job, of Sarah, the lesson from the Last Sup-

per, in fact, the entire life of Jesus, would have us believe that humankind must, in the face of great odds and social approbation, find and follow the right path. It is too easy to suggest that we should play the hand dealt to us. May I suggest that too often we have not looked at our cards carefully enough? I have; I have found a wild card in the hand; and I intend to play it.

I recall that in a separate conversation you suggested that God placed each of us on this earth for a reason; although I cannot subscribe to that belief, I simply wish to counter that, in that context, perhaps my reason for being here is to have the operation, to change my life in this manner, so that I can demonstrate to others that if I can take such an action, then they can take smaller actions which their fear or society has, until now, prevented them from taking. But I cannot argue this line to long; it runs against my grain.

My actions are mine, and yours are yours, and their interactions are random and undirected. The excitement comes from working through those interactions . . . Finally, you ask if there is a possibility that I have mistaken my attraction to women for wanting to be one. Perhaps my desire does flow from my lifelong love of women, but this cause and effect concern you raise here (and elsewhere) is not of interest to me. Would it matter if you knew why your son has little *interest at present to certain things you hold dear? The cause is unimportant, the effect is the element you wish to comprehend and perhaps modify.*

I began plans for July and I drafted a letter to send to some 250 administrators here at the University. I planned on transitioning in July, and I planned to release the letter two months before that.

In early March, however, I started to get feedback that there was a rumor going around campus that I was going to do this—however, the rumor was low-key and isolated to certain parts. In mid-March, I got a call from a trusted friend that the rumor was everywhere and was spreading off campus. The next day, I met with my boss, my senior staff, and the following day I had a group meeting with my twenty clerical staff. I told each of my decision, handed them a copy of the yet to be issued letter explaining everything, and allowed plenty of time for reaction. At the clerical meeting, I had a Ph.D. clinical psychologist with me.

The letter was then sent to the administrators:

March 19, 1993

To: The President, Vice Presidents, Deans, Assistant Deans, Chairs, and Directors

From: Peter Rachael, Director of Business Services

There is no good way to begin this letter except to say that on July 6, I will begin living my life as a woman. My name will be legally Kristen, and to all intents and purposes, on that date, Peter will no longer legally exist.

I suffer from a condition called gender dysphoria. Simply put, my gender does not align with my genetic sex. This is not an acquired condition; rather, it is an intrinsic part, a lifelong aspect of my being. It is a rare condition, to be sure, but one extensively studied and with a generally accepted medical treatment.

There is no easy way to explain to you the basis for this condition or decision, nor can I expect that you will completely understand the full nature of how I feel. In fact, medical and mental health professionals with extensive education, training and experience in this area do not truly know how their patients feel.

The influences which cause a person to develop this conflict between their gender and their biologically determined sex can be described and pre- or post-natal (pre- or post-birth). Current research indicates that the most likely pre-natal cause for gender dysphoria can be found in certain hormonal imbalances at a critical point in the development of the fetus. The result is that an individual can develop having the anatomical features of one sex while having the gender of the other.

Post-natal influences on gender dysphoria are typically believed to come from family structure and attitudes and certain societal responses to gender typing. However, it is simply not possible to say that a certain type of childhood experience will result in gender dysphoria. In fact, studies show that gender dysphoric individuals, in general, have a childhood that is more similar to that experienced by most other children than it is dissimilar (both in its positive and negative experiences).

Over time, various solutions have been suggested by the medical and mental health communities to resolve this conflict, but the only one that has been found to be effective to date is for the individual to live as their gender rather than as their biological sex.

I became aware of my female gender identity at about the age of four. I have spent a good part of my life struggling with this conflict between my body and my mind. I have studied this subject in depth, I have been treated by professionals, but I have also spent a great deal of time and effort hiding, denying and trying, to no avail, to be "normal," to purge my female gender identity.

Finally, I gradually came to accept that my gender dysphoria is part of who I am as a person; it is part of the reality of my being. I have slowly followed a course of action to find peace and harmony and comfort with my gender. On July 6, my biological birthday, I will effect the physical birthday of the gender I wish to have for the rest of my life.

Since making the decision, I have found an inner peace that I have never felt before, but I know that the foreseeable future will be a time of great stress for me. And I know there will be stress for some of you.

Sex is a rigid barrier for most of us, and to see someone crossing that boundary is disconcerting. I have no desire to cause feelings of discomfort in anyone, but I hope some of you will find a way to tolerate my decision even if you cannot endorse it. I have chosen to make the announcement of my plans in this public manner, and at this time, so as to allow people to work through the implications of what I am doing, and, if they wish, to discuss the matter with me well before the transition date I have chosen. This has not been an easy letter to write, and it probably has not been an easy letter for you to read. Over the past few months, I have told a small number of friends of my decision, and in doing so, I have learned that people need time to work through the implications of what I have told them, to place my decision in their own terms. I have also learned that people typically have many questions to ask.

The success of my transition will depend on my being open and honest with everyone, and this is the reason for this letter. I am more than willing to answer any and all questions you might have, and I invite you, if you wish, to call me or to discuss the matter with me in person. There are no "dumb" questions as they relate to gender dysphoria; I had to research this for years, and I still do not understand all of it.

I want to conclude by thanking those of you who welcomed Peter several years ago when I returned to my native state from "away," and I hope you will be able to accept Kristen in the future.

I waited for the explosion; none came.

Rather, I started to get calls of support and notes of support. The President and each Vice President wrote, as did people I didn't know.

But this was four months before I planned to transition. Too much time for people to get worked up. Two weeks after the memo went out, I got a call from the local newspaper (only two in the state), saying that they were going to do a story on me, quoting from my memo. I fought it, quoting anonymity, but they felt I was a public figure. I finally agreed to an interview to hope to put a human face on the "freak" article, but then wrote the following to the editor:

Ms. Joan Smith
Editor, Style Section
Daily News
Dear Ms. Smith:

As you know, I reluctantly agreed to be interviewed by Tom Weber about my planned gender change when I learned that the **Daily News** *intended to do a story with or without my "permission." By allowing an interview, I hoped to minimize the likelihood of a negative article. However, as I explained to you, I felt, and still do, that the matter of my gender change is not an appropriate subject to appear in a newspaper.*

At the least, the article is an invasion of my privacy; at the worst, its publication smacks of sensationalism.

On the issue of privacy, it is true that I notified many members of the University community of my plans, but unlike your readership, members of the University must work with me each day and they need to decide how my change will affect them. This is not the case with your readership; very few who were ignorant of my plans before your article will have to deal with me; absolutely none need to know of my change.

On the issue of sensationalism, I ask whether you would have run the article if I had worked for a private firm instead of the university, or if my problem had been, instead, AIDS, cancer, or mental illness. Likewise, I wonder why you did not consent to running the article without using my name or work affiliation.

Certainly, this article has made a private matter intensely public; I will have to suffer the consequences of your decision to publish the article. And sadly, so will that portion of your readership which suffers from sexual identity questions or other prob-lems, since each will fear that his or her private life, like mine, could become fodder for the Daily News.

Peter Rachael

March 31, 1993

The letter apparently worked—although she did not agree to kill the article, she agreed to run it anonymously. Except, they forgot to delete one reference to the University—and they ran an enormous picture of me.

It was in their weekend edition, which is distributed throughout the state, and the article was next to Dave Barry's column. Rather appropriate, I thought.

Reprinted without permission, but who cares—they were going to quote from my memo without my permission.

A SEARCH FOR GENDER IDENTITY

After a lifetime of feeling he was a woman trapped in a man's body, a sex change was the answer he chose

(Editor's note—At the interviewee's request, names have been changed.)

By Tom Weber; News Senior Writer

After more than 40 years of unhappiness and confusion, of feeling so at odds with himself and the world that suicide seemed to be the only solution, Scot decided to radically alter his life.

He explained his decision on March 19 in a letter to 250 employees of the large institution where he has worked for two years. Having wrestled for weeks with the proper wording, he chose an opening paragraph guaranteed to raise more than a few eyebrows and questions:

"There is no good way to begin this letter except to say that on July 6, I will be living my life as a woman. My name will be legally Kristin Rachael, and to all intents and purposes, on that date, Scot will no longer legally exist."

With the letter in circulation, he waited for the storm of protest that he supposed would follow so startling an announcement. Yet instead of losing his high-ranking position, a possibility he anticipated, he received a letter of support from his boss.

Claiming that as long as Scot's performance and health remained satisfactory, and the performance of those who worked with him was not adversely affected, his boss and he looked forward to working with Scot, regardless of his gender.

While some of Scot's friends and colleagues found his decision to be morally troubling and even bizarre, their responses so far have been more compassionate than hostile.

"I care what happens to Scot. He's a human being and a kind person," said Donna, who works for Scot. "But it's hard to believe this is going to make him happy. I'm afraid what my reaction will be when he walks into the office with a dress on. This state, or at least this part of the state, may not be ready for this."

Scot, who said he expected anger and frustration, is delighted about the support and understanding he has received.

"I'm pleased to say that I've had some very good responses, even a nice letter," he said recently at his office. "I have yet to get a negative letter, but I expect it.

Sex is a rigid barrier for most of us, and to see someone crossing that boundary is disconcerting."

"Many people thought I was a homosexual—I'm not. When those people saw me dating women, they knew it was more complex. But the sexual part is not the issue here. It's the last thing on my mind. I'm not doing this to have sex with men, but to live the life I've always wanted."

Born in Portland in 1947, the oldest of four children, Scot said he sensed at the age of four that something was wrong with him.

"Even then I was conscious of being uncomfortable with my body," said Scot, who wore a white shirt, tie, dress slacks, a touch of mascara and a flouncy elastic securing his ponytail. "I had dreams of being a girl, and enjoyed playing more with my younger sister than with the boys in the neighborhood. I thought that if I just believed, I would grow up to be a girl, it would happen. Of course it didn't."

His largely unhappy childhood evolved into pubescent crisis. Not only was he attracted to girls, he wanted to be one—to incorporate in himself those very female qualities he found so desirable. At a private all-male school in Massachusetts, Scot attempted suicide for the first time. He was kicked out. After intensive psychotherapy, during which he was introduced to his baffling condition known as "gender dysphoria," he returned to the school and graduated with high honors.

"Therapy taught me coping mechanisms, though I was never reconciled to my gender," he said.

Scot got a bachelor's degree in 1969 from the University of Chicago. Two years later, after having dated "a string of girlfriends" in college, he got married. Scot said that 60 percent of transsexuals such as himself do, in fact, have heterosexual relationships. While Scot's wife knew he liked to dress in women's clothing, she asked only that he not do it in her presence.

"I was married for 15 years," he said. "There was a strain on the marriage, sure, but it wasn't an issue of great concern. The marriage broke up not because of the gender dysphoria, but because we were both professionals and moved our separate ways. We had no children."

After receiving a doctorate in educational administration, Scot forged a successful career at the University of Chicago. Two years ago, tired of the city life that caused him to become cold and uncaring, he moved back here to take his present job.

A year ago, still desperately struggling with his "gender identity," he tried to kill himself for the second time. After surviving yet another suicide attempt last November, Scot said, he knew he could not continue living in denial. He would finally have to undergo the sex-change operation that would join his warring physical and emotional selves.

"I came to the critical point and decided there would never be a good time to do it, that now was a good time," he said. "I reviewed all the possibilities—that I could lose my job, my friends, my home. But I had no choice. This couldn't be counselled out of me."

Before going public with his letter, Scot assembled his clerical staff to gauge their reaction to his plan. The employees were from small rural towns, many with families whose roots in this area ran deep. One woman asked Scot why he decided to undergo his dramatic transformation here, and not in a more anonymous setting like Boston or New York.

"I asked her what her reaction would be if her husband said he was being transferred to Connecticut, and that she would be cut off from all she knew," Scot said. "It's the same for me. When I came here two years ago, I had friends, a house. I've put down roots here, too, and I'm loathe to pull them up. Now, for the first time in my life, I feel like a whole person."

On the morning of July 6, his 46th birthday, Scot will choose a female business outfit from his closet, do his hair and makeup and walk into the office as a woman named Kristin. He has already begun the electrolysis that he hopes will have smoothed his face by then. The female hormones he has been taking since November will eventually soften the angularity of his slender body.

He said he will feel terribly self-conscious when greeting his employees at first, just as they will feel uncomfortable greeting their boss.

"It will bother me," Donna said. "I just can't imagine him as a woman. I will respect him, as I do now, but I really think he's going to make himself more of an outcast than he feels he is already."

Eliot, a data-processing coordinator who works next-door to Scot, said his religious beliefs will never allow him to accept his boss's decision. Yet Eliot said he, too, will continue to respect Scot for his skills and professionalism he has always brought to the work place.

"I'm a Jehovah's Witness, so in a personal way I feel this goes against what is natural," Eliot said. "But will it impact what I do here? No, I have developed a lot of respect for what he's done here. We're good business partners. So whether he is in a male's outfit or a female's doesn't make any difference to me. I don't think this has a negative effect on the university."

If, after a year of living as a woman, he is still determined to take the next crucial step, Scot will go to either Colorado, Wisconsin, or Canada to undergo the surgery that will give him—within anatomical limits—a woman's body. After that, he said, the process he should have begun years ago will have been completed.

"Would I have wished for a different life if I could do it over again? Well, this has been a part of me for so long, I couldn't imagine it not being this way," he said. "If I could have pushed a button 20 years ago and lived a normal life, and not have gone through the grief, I would have. On the other hand, I wouldn't push that button now. Finally, I am able to change my gender and damn it, I'm going to do it."

In early April, three months to the Real Life Test (RLT), the period of living as a woman, the real grief begins. Several members of my clerical staff are agitating against me (Why are you putting us through this; why do we have to quit our jobs if we can't take your appearance after July 6; why doesn't the University make you leave?) And then, Donna, the woman quoted twice in the article, and an employee of mine, decides to fall in love with me—and doesn't want me to go ahead with my plans.

July 1993

Real ups and downs all spring. Donna is making my life both great and miserable, the staff continues to agitate, I get tired of the time I have to wait, especially as I read on Transgen of people who decide one day and transition two weeks later.

When I believed I was a transvestite (TV), I never saw in the mirror anything but "...a guy in makeup..." But, and here is the strange thing, after I made the decision in November to go for the RLT, I did not get completely dressed up once. At the time, I rationalized it away by saying that I was going to hold off until the big day. In fact, I think I was worried that I would continue to see just "a guy in makeup" and I would chicken out of the RLT.

In making the decision for the RLT, I had told myself that, no matter what I looked like on July 6, that was the life I was going to lead. After all, I had made the decision because I could no longer live as Peter. He wasn't then, and never really had been the whole me.

So, it was an absolutely incredible thing when, on the first day of the RLT, I dressed up, put on my makeup, did my hair and faced the world.

For the first time, this was real, and because of this it did not matter to me that I wasn't good looking. (Don't we sometimes use as an excuse for not transitioning that we will never be as good looking as we wish we could be.) However, on that first day, looking back at me was the face and body of an average woman, and I smiled.

But, a step back.

By the beginning of July, I had gone through 180 hours of electrolysis, six hours of private makeup lessons, and, of course, countless hours of psychotherapy. (As someone advised me early on, get your act together before your change, because after the change it is sometimes hard to separate change issues from non-change issues.)

I had also purchased more clothes than my savings account could safely cover. Early on, I had decided that, after years of wearing men's clothes, I would never wear women's business suits. So, after twenty-five years of admiring the taste of career women in Chicago, I found my taste running to upscale "career" dressing.

July 6 actually arrived as these things have a tendency to do. After taking the 40 minute drive from my home to campus and parking my car in the lot, I checked myself out in the mirror, adjusted my handbag, grabbed my bottled water and walked into work. I had already decided that I would not alter my daily routine, and so, as I do every morning, I said hello to each of my employees, and then I went about my day as if I had always been Kristin. As usual, I went to the student union for lunch, and I took a walk across the campus in the mid afternoon. In short, I acted as if the day were a normal one, and I hoped people would act the same. As several had suggested, I always acted confidently and did not make as much eye contact with others as some men are apt to do.

And things went incredibly well. Even the employee who I knew was having the biggest problem with my change came into my office soon after I arrived and she wished me well. Other staff members clearly found the change jolting, but they continued to treat me in a professional way. However, something started to surprise me: those who knew me and knew of my change looked at me and even commented, but the many who didn't know me acted as if nothing were wrong—that is, they seemed to believe that I was, indeed, a woman. I naturally assumed they were being polite, because I just knew that I must have a big sign on my front and back saying "man in a dress, look away!"

So, later in the week, I did the real test and went to Wal-Mart and to a busy supermarket. I expected the gawkers and the whispering, but they never came. Oh sure, I did catch a few double takes, but after the second look, the expected gawking did not occur. Maybe the second look was just to satisfy the person that this six-foot, slender woman was, indeed, exactly what she appeared to be. So, either there is an incredible agreement amongst the entire population of my home town that they will act as if there is nothing unusual about a "man in a dress," or I must be presenting just enough of the necessary visual and body language signals, so that their subconscious minds accept those signals as female, and do not send the dreaded "check out that person" message to interrupt the conscious mind's weighty contemplation of when the heat will break, or how the Red Sox are doing.

When I stopped by my hairdresser to change my appointment, she didn't recognize me at first, and at a ribbon-cutting ceremony later in the week, two of my "fellow" administrators stood beside me for five minutes and seemingly reacted with honest surprise when I said hello.

Fall 1993

So now, it is months later, and the good and the bad continues. Several members of my staff continue to give me grief, Donna continues to try to make me pull back, and there is always the fear of being "read" in public, but I have come to grips with that.

I know that one of my greatest fears was the ridicule I believed I would face transitioning openly, in a rural

115

state, in a job of relative visibility, in an academic setting.

I sometimes wonder if we fail to realize how wide is the range of female appearance. In agonizing over whether to change, I know that I filtered my perceptions through the cultural stereotype of the beautiful woman. It was when I realized that I could no longer be Peter that I no longer cared how I would end up looking.

Allison L., in one of her videotapes, said something that made me pause and rerun the segment. She said that she doesn't worry about passing; she simply wants to be accepted as a woman, i.e. the waitress, the town clerk, the person at the DMV, may know full well that we are not genetic women, but the important thing is that we are accepted and treated with due respect.

Certainly, passing is important, but acceptance is especially important for those of us who are doing our RLT in full view of those who knew us in our male personas. With these people, it is not an issue of passing; many will never see us without that little voice in their head saying, "that is really Peter." But while they may not be able to accept us as genetic women, if they no longer see us as male, then we have won much of the battle.

But we must also do things to help them accept us as women.

A friend wrote to me telling me how difficult it was to get her colleagues to accept her as a woman. I suggested that she wear to work only dresses and skirts for three weeks—i.e., no slacks. She found it made a difference; they needed help in making the mental transition from her male persona to her female persona.

Oh, I am not saying that we cannot wear slacks, jeans, etc. Nor am I saying that we should dress as if we were going to the theater when we are just going out to breakfast. What I am simply saying is that, during the RLT, it became real, at least for me, because I was fostering an environment in which people, and I myself, could see me as a woman and not simply as "a guy in makeup." We need to give them enough gender signals so their subconscious minds can read us as women, or if we do not spend that much time with our image, at least not register anything that will cause the second look.

But as I noted, acceptance is also critical. I spent a Sunday afternoon recently in a bar in a fishing village, the bar filled with rowdy fishermen who, because of the gale winds, had been unable to venture out into the cold Atlantic. Some "read" me or perhaps wondered. The majority didn't, but no one seemed to care. No snickering, no sideways glances. (Oh, no, I don't usually hang out in such locations, they happen to make great fish chowder, and that was just what I wanted on a damp, wind-driven gray Sunday.)

January 1994

I now have a date for surgery: May 26 in Neenah, Wisconsin with Dr. Eugene Schrang, perhaps the best SRS surgeon in the U.S. Too many people view the surgery as the primary event; with the proper attitude, the surgery is just a rest stop on the journey. If the goal is to change gender, to be who we have wished and needed to be for years, then the RLT is the big event. To the public we are women upon beginning the RLT. Most do not know we have not had the surgery; those who do know quickly forget and then are surprised when they hear it has been done a year or two later.

But I am pursuing surgery.

Why?

Because I have chosen to live the rest of my life as a woman, and a woman does not have a penis.

Society believes gender is absolute; much of the society around me would have me remain a man. Those people think it would be so much easier for them if I remained a man.

By entering into the RLT, I am refusing to accept society's dictates. I am saying that I have a right to live the life I choose, not the life society chose for me based on a chromosomal count.

When I have the SRS, the effect will also be to deny society's petty definition of what is right or wrong.

However, and this is important, that is not the reason for my SRS.

I am not going through the RLT or SRS to teach society anything.

I am doing this for myself. Society can take any lesson it wishes from my life.

SRS will just be a footnote to my RLT; it will simply bring part of my body in line with my self image.

Much of society will not even know when I have the surgery.

But I will.

Kristin

March 30, 1994

Re: Kristen Rachael

Dear Dr. Schrang,

Thank you for referring Dr. Kristen Rachael to me for a consultation.

Kristen is an extremely intelligent, 46 year-old male to female transsexual who holds a Ph.D. degree in education. She is presently employed as the Director of Business Services for a large University. She attended the University of Chicago, and had a rather illustrious career teaching English literature at the University of Kent in England. She was married for 15 years, and would have continued her idyllic existence in England, if it were not for the gender identity disorder that plagued her throughout her lifetime.

Like most transsexuals, Kristen gives a history of dressing in girl's clothing at a very early age, and expressing the wish to be a girl. After her first date, Kristen attempted suicide, as she realized how unsuited she was for normal male activities. During her marriage, she often faked ejaculation to maintain the pretense that she was "normal."

As the depressive episodes became more frequent and more intractable, Kristen knew she must become the female she was within the deepest recesses of her mind. She began hormones and transitioned, which brought her unwanted notoriety in her small town.

She has consulted with Dr. Fred Ettner regarding her hormonal treatment. She is an insightful, kind and respectful person who asks only respect in return. Again, thank you for referring her to me.

Sincerely, Dr. Randi Ettner

Dear Randi:

Again, I wish to thank you for the delightful time I spent with you in March. As I indicated at the beginning of the conversation, my anticipation of the consultation was heightened by the several long phone calls we had shared and by my knowledge that I would have the opportunity to spend some time with an educated and intelligent professional—something that is sadly lacking in my life since I left the University of Chicago.

I have been thinking about our conversation regarding the fact that transsexuals have no advocacy group, unlike, say, gay men or lesbian women. Indeed we do not, and I think we both agree that this works to our detriment in many ways. However, I doubt whether one shall ever exist, for, unlike gay men or lesbian women, transsexuals, I believe, wish to live in society on society's terms. That is, after my surgery in three weeks, my ideal would be to live in society as if I had been born a woman. The last thing I wish to have happen is for those I associate with to have at the front or even the back of their minds the thought that I was born male. The transsexual, pre- or post-op, wishes, I believe, to be "invisible." In contrast, I believe most gay men or lesbian women wish to have their sexual choice accepted as part of life's rich diversity. "Gay Pride" events, are, I think, the best manifestation of this: participants are saying that they are proud of who they are.

The transsexual, however, has no such pride, wishing to be something other than he or she was born. Nor, upon achieving surgical congruity, does the transsexual have a pride that can be shared with others, for to do so would be to acknowledge that, post-op, they are still different from the men or women they have joined. I recall reading an account of African-Americans who are able to pass as white; while perhaps satisfied with being able to do so, they could not share this feeling with others, for to do so would expose that they were not, indeed, what people took them for.

So, while there will be articulate pre- and post-op transsexuals able to discuss our wishes and needs with the larger society, I feel there can never be a collective transsexual consciousness or pride. Even now, I find myself withdrawing from the various e-mail groups which helped me in this journey, partially because of the pain of some early in the journey reminds me too much of my own past, but primarily because my concern now is simply to be Kristen.

But enough hot air.

Again, many thanks, and as I fly over Chicago I will wave in your direction.

Sincerely, Kristen Rachael

Dear Randi:

As we have discussed, I hereby grant permission to you to quote from all of the material I have sent or will send you regarding my "journey" from Peter to Kristen and beyond. This permission is granted without limitation of use or time.

I would appreciate it if you could change any references to my home state to "a rural northern state" or simply "a rural state." I think my experiences are very different from those experienced by my friends in the cities, but, by my specification of "northern," I believe they are also quite different from the experiences of my friends in the rural South.

The Yankee mindset seems to allow coexistence with behavior at variance to the norm if such behavior does not infringe upon the "normal" individual's own perceived rights. In contrast, my friend, who is a professor at a university in the Deep South, is waging an ongoing battle against those in the Bible-belt who feel that any behavior at variance to the norm is not only sinful, but confers to the "normal" individual a god-given right to publicly condemn or drive out the "sinner."

Sincerely, Kristen

FOR BETTER OR FOR WORSE

By the time she was twenty-seven years old, she had been married twice, divorced twice, and was the mother of three small children. Linda was working two jobs, trying to stay off welfare. Each day began and ended with a steady stream of babysitters. Life was no bed of roses.

It was January, 1979, in a small town in Oklahoma, when Linda first met Gary. He worked in the hotel gift shop where she waitressed. Often, Linda would drop by and chat. But she was cautious, very cautious. After all, one gets wary after two bad marriages. If Linda had learned anything it was that men are not what they appear to be on the surface. But there was something different about Gary. He was gentle and sensitive, and after three months Linda let down her guard, and agreed to go out with him. She was buying a used car and Gary convinced her to let him go with her for a test drive. Linda says they've been test driving ever since.

She is seated across from me, narrating her life. I'm surveying her face. It's as round and as sweet as an apple pie. I'm thinking that when I lay dying in some hospital, of some caffeine-induced disease, I hope this lady is my nurse. She is both sprightly and yet "no-nonsense." Perfect qualities for a nurse.

Eight months of courtship and Linda marries Gary. Turns out Gary is different from other guys. Gary seems determined to help Linda grow as a human being. He doesn't view her as a "sex object," either. In fact, he wouldn't spend the night during those eight months of courtship because Linda had children in the house and he didn't think it was right. "He convinced me to go to nursing school. He kept telling me over and over I could do something with my life. He paid my tuition, babysat my kids, and bought my books."

Linda is grinning as she tells me this. I watch the skinny, cheerful crows feet jog up and down her eyelids as she smiles and recounts the early days.

"We paid for our own wedding. He flew my mom in from Utah. My mom and Gary's mom spent our wedding night in my mobile home with my kids. We spent our wedding night in his mom's mobile home."

Gary was so enthusiastic about Linda's decision to start nursing school, and so enthusiastic about Linda, that he enrolled also, and they went to school together. This was a kind of love she had only dreamed of. Her youngest child was four years old. That little boy learned the bones of the arms and the legs when most kids were learning fingers and toes. Two and a half years later Linda and Gary graduated. The first thing they did was to buy a piece of land in Guthrie, Oklahoma and clear it. They moved the mobile home there so the children would have more room to grow. Now they were Gary's children, too, and he loved them fiercely.

Linda and Gary took jobs in various local hospitals. In the early years they had the usual marital problems—money and the kids.

"How did you and Gary deal with conflict in your marriage?" I ask.

"Gary and I always worked things out. We never really argued. But we always would discuss and compromise. We made sure one of us wasn't always giving in. That way we were both halfway happy all the time. I'd give in one time, Gary would give in the next. And we never let the kids play us against one another. We made them ask permission in front of both of us so we could jointly decide. During the teenage years they'd tell Gary they didn't have to mind him cause he wasn't their real father, but they got over that pretty quick."

The thing that saved Gary, when Linda found out that he was a transsexual, was this ability to compromise:

"Linda wasn't looking for a white knight who could solve her problems. I had helped her become an independent woman. I always read and heard from the cross-dressing community that if you tell your wife after the marriage about your gender problems, the marriage is over. That's why I didn't tell her for so many years. That, and my hope that my love for her would 'cure' me."

Gary knew forever—ever since he knew the difference between boys and girls. He knew he was more comfortable with the girls. His brother, a clergyman, remembered a picture of him dressed as a girl. Gary didn't remember the picture, but he'll never forget the beating. Another time, Gary recalls, in sixth grade, there was trouble with a teacher:

"I wanted to take dancing with the girls. The boys were supposed to play basketball. The teacher was insistent that I join the boys. My grandmother taught me to knit . . . My dad found the knitting and tore it up. In college, I took gym in the women's physical education department: dance. They actually allowed me to take a dance class! I was the only boy in the class, but I felt comfortable."

Like many transsexuals, Gary would cross-dress when possible, even if it only meant wearing women's underwear, which no one could detect. Unlike many, who buy clothes and "purge" them, Gary knew the desire to "dress" wouldn't go away. He kept the clothes. The dress and purge cycle is a common one in the history of people with gender conditions. The urge to dress builds up and when one finally gives in and dresses, there is a tremendous feeling of relaxation or inner peace. Later however, this feeling is outstripped by the pervasive guilt of having done something so "perverse" or unnatural. In a moment of remorse and self-loathing, the cross-dresser disposes of the clothing, vowing never to dress again. Many people have told me they have purged themselves of numerous, extensive, wardrobes throughout their lifetime.

In 1990 Gary was managing a company, due to a shortage of nursing positions. He was sent to Chicago for a three day training seminar. When he arrived, the men in his group went directly to the clubs, looking for action. Gary sat in his hotel room, painstakingly shaving his beard off. Then, he went out and bought himself a wig and a nice dress. Next stop: makeup. Even so, Gary looked awful. It was Gary's first time "out" in public. All the dressing before had been furtive, behind bedroom doors when Linda was working night shifts. He didn't "pass" as a female, but he spent three nights in that raiment. Three glorious nights. Then something happened. It was an epiphany for Gary. Sitting in that dingy hotel room with stained carpeting, he realized that the "woman" he saw in the mirror was his true self. This was not something he was doing for kicks.

When Gary left this retreat in Chicago and returned home, he had made a major life decision. He decided he had "better learn something about this." He had access to computers, so he started with the gay bulletin boards. But, Linda's oldest son was gay, and Gary knew that wasn't "him." He couldn't be gay if he didn't feel like a man himself and if he wasn't attracted to men, he reasoned. Finally, he ran across something on the bulletin boards under the header of "gender." That fit. Gary spent the next two years downloading information. He longed to talk face to face to someone in a similar situation, but couldn't find any support groups in the Tulsa area. He had to settle for electronic empathy.

And all the while the urge to dress grew stronger and stronger. It became harder to hide articles of clothing. Gary rented a storage area, and dressed frequently. As frequently as he could that is, without being discovered by Linda.

There is a tendency in Western societies, to confuse sex with gender. They are truly different concepts.

Sex, to differentiate it from gender, can be thought of as erotic desires or activity. Gender can best be thought of as maleness or femaleness. Most people are assumed to "belong" to a category of gender, determined solely on the basis of their genitals. So, the doctor raises the newborn from the perineum, makes a cursory examination of the pubic region, and proclaims this newborn either "boy" or "girl." In the majority of cases, this bifurcation may be appropriate. That is to say, that most individual humans born with a penis and scrotum would readily identify themselves as males. Moreover, they are truly comfortable with this designation. They perceive themselves suited for the roles society assigns them, such as fathering, etc., and might very well describe themselves as "masculine." In truth, gender is more appropriately conceptualized as a continuum, rather than two distinct categories. No one is totally masculine, nor totally feminine. Therefore, this binary classification system fails miserably in addressing the disposition of the minority group of individuals who fit into a category inconsistent with their natal assignment, or into no category at all.

The transsexual raises many questions about the social constructs of gender. If one were to ask the male who wants to have reassignment what they mean when they say they "feel female" their answer might be less about femininity than congruity. Femininity is, after all very culturally dependent. It is not so much what the transsexual *is* as what they are *not.* It is the absence of identification with maleness that causes these individuals to seek a gender transition. They feel as though their body is a "shell" and they are being related to by society as though they were the shell.

Gary was no "different" in terms of his behavior when he came "out." He merely felt comfortable. He was free to spend more time with women in conversations. He didn't have to pretend to be interested in sports or assume the male roles that society attributes to men. His pursuit of femaleness was, in essence, a flight from masculinity.

The mental health professional who works with individuals with gender conditions can best avoid confusion by equating the individual's innermost self-perception as the true gender. This means it is appropriate to refer to the transsexual as "she" in the case of the male-to-female-transsexual, and "he" in the case of the female-to male, and using the preferred chosen name. In other words, the clinician must realize that even though the person who is consulting with him may look masculine, (often very much so) nevertheless, they are female. Their psyche, "soul," nature, or orientation to the world is more female than male.

Now, consider the following: Just as "genetic" men or women can be either heterosexual or homosexual, so too, can the transsexual be of either of these aforementioned orientations. A transsexual can be a lesbian. In other words, a man, who makes a gender transition, and becomes outwardly as female as inwardly, can be attracted to either males or females. The gender of the individual, again, is separate from whom they feel a sexual attraction to. It has been estimated that 30% of transsexuals are homosexual.

It must be noted, that while sexual preference can change, gender is constant. A man may marry, father children, have sexual reassignment, and find that rather than being attracted to females, as a female "she" is attracted to males. But the authentic gender of an individual remains consistent, even if the individual denies awareness of it.

It is not uncommon for a person, when they begin to acknowledge their gender problems, to assume that perhaps they are "just" a gay man. Often people in the process of discovery will experiment with gay sexual encounters. Some will just frequent gay bars to try to see if they are in their "comfort zone." Most often, the transsexual becomes very clear that they are not a gay man and they definitively rule out that possibility.

After twelve wonderful years, the honeymoon was over. Linda didn't know what changed, but something was different between her and Gary. Gary had been on a three day business trip to Chicago, and when he came back, he seemed troubled and remote. For the first time in their marriage there was a "wall" between them. Gary was still gentle and kind, but the closeness that had made their relationship unique was gone. They seemed to be in two different worlds with little communication between the two.

Bit by bit the relationship began to unravel. Linda was particularly saddened by the fact that she and Gary had struggled so hard to get to this stage of life, and now they were coming undone. With the kids finally grown, and the bills paid, they were free to enjoy each other. But was there anything left to enjoy? Linda wondered.

They took a cruise. Leaving Tulsa for a while might be good therapy. On board, the social director announced a "male nightgown contest." Gary entered the contest. But something unusual occurred. Linda didn't think much of it at the time, but later she would recall it and attach great significance to it. Gary shaved his arms, his legs, his back and his chest.

January 19, 1993, is a day that Linda will never forget. On that day, which began much like any other day, Linda was cleaning house. She found, while putting away Gary's laundry, a small book hidden among his belongings. It looked like a diary. Curious, Linda opened it. At first she was extremely puzzled, for the title page read, in typeset, "Diary of Glenda Allison." Linda sifted through her memory, trying to recall if Gary had a relative by the name of Glenda, or if they had ever known anyone by that name.

Slowly, she lowered herself to the bed. Still clutching the little book in her hands, she read the first entry. Suddenly, the room began to spin, and Linda was trying desperately to breathe. She realized she was losing consciousness, and put her head between her knees to stymie the vagus reflex. The handwriting was Gary's!

It's hard to tell your wife that you're a transsexual. If you tell her before you marry, obviously she'll abandon you. If you tell her after the marriage, she'll divorce you in a New York minute.

Some males do in fact confide to their fiances that they like to occasionally sport women's clothing. Some women can tolerate this, with assurances by the partner that it will never go any farther than bedroom dress-up.

For some, it doesn't go any farther. Those individuals, commonly referred to as transvestites, do enjoy wearing clothing, but don't have the desire to change their sex, or the revulsion of their genitals. They are predominately heterosexual males.

For many years the psychiatric community thought of transvestites as fetishists; men who are sexually aroused by articles of women's clothing. Currently, this view is changing. Dr. Leah Schaefer is past president of the Harry Benjamin International Gender Dysphoria Association, an organization of professionals who specialize in gender conditions, rejects this definition. According to Dr. Schaefer, transvestitism has nothing to do with fetishism. The pleasure derived from dressing has to do with the individual's perception of oneself as female. It is an identity issue, not a sexual issue.

The difference between transvestitism and transsexualism is that the former appears later in life, around adolescence, rather than in early childhood, as with the transsexual. Because it appears later, developmentally speaking, it doesn't have the same intensity, the power to compel one to completely change their physical persona. Fundamentally, though, both conditions have the same etiologic origins.

For the transsexual, unlike the transvestite, the anguish of being in the wrong body takes a cumulative toll. Eventually, many dissolve their partnerships, concluding that married life is hopeless. Others, reveal themselves to their spouses, in the hopes that they can still maintain the integrity of the family.

There is no formula for conveying this information to a spouse. Individuals are cautioned by therapists to broach the subject slowly, though. No one can expect a partner to assimilate such emotionally-loaded confessions in bulk. We generally advise the patient to begin by talking in generalities about people who cross-dress, and gauging their partner's reaction. They are encouraged to slowly, over the course of many conversations, begin to reveal their feelings and relate them to their gender condition.

Having professional support is very helpful during this process. There will be many misconceptions to clear up, including how this condition differs from homosexuality and transvestitism. It is crucial that the gender dysphoric individual show the utmost sensitivity to their spouse at this time. It is essential that they avoid overwhelming their partner and creating flat-out rejection which may be impossible to counteract later on.

Most wives react to the information, predictably, with shock, horror, and anxiety. This initial reaction is often followed by anger at having "been deceived," feelings of being out of control, and extreme fear of the future. For many women, it triggers anxiety about their own identity and sexuality. "If you're telling me that you feel like a female, that makes me a lesbian!"

For some women, the news of the husband's gender dysphoria may come as no surprise. Many women find telltale clues, such as missing undergarments or items secreted in the recesses of the closet, that verify this inference. Some of these wives are understanding, but nevertheless, want what they consider to be "real red-blooded" men for partners.

One client of mine dated his wife for six years before their marriage. He describes their premarital relationship as "wonderful . . . we were really like best friends." In his desire to be absolutely candid with her, he told her that he often cross-dressed and even had feelings of wishing he were a woman. His girlfriend seemed understanding. After this six year courtship, this individual went to a counselor to explore these gender issues and make some decisions as to how to live his life. The counselor knew nothing about cross-dressing or gender conditions, and after four sessions the young man left treatment.

Feeling confused and conflicted, he married his girlfriend in a June wedding. For two months everything seemed okay. He assumed the gender role of "husband" and tried to convince himself that this was "working." However, he grew noticeably depressed. His spouse and friends were concerned about him. He seemed totally uninterested in sexual relations with his wife. Finally, he once again opened up to his wife about his feelings, in the fifth month of their marriage. "Remember the feelings I told you about before, my wanting to be a woman?" His wife told him that she thought he had "worked through" that in therapy and moved out the very next day, never to see him again.

Some wives, particularly where there are growing children in the family, try to set limits on the spouse's expression of femininity. Some prohibit the husband from dressing or wearing makeup at home. Some draw the line at hormones. Hormone usage attenuates the ability to achieve or maintain an erection; an important consideration for intimate life. Some wives grieve over the loss of the "hairy chest and arms" that occurs with body shaving and hormones. Many divorce their husbands and try to rebuild their lives, but maintain continuing friendships with their former spouses.

Then there are the exceptions. These women are a breed apart. This group have one thing in common: they don't feel threatened by the thought of living with someone of the same sex. They do not tend to personalize the partner's gender problem; rather they sympathize. Many have high self-esteem. They often attend support groups for spouses and try to accommodate their partner's "revised" view of themselves.

For some this leads to very creative living configurations. For example, some transsexuals stay married to their spouse and live together as two women. If questioned as to why they have the same last name, they might give the explanation that they are sisters-in-law.

Happily married couples often find that the mosaic of their lives together, like ficus trees braided together as cuttings, are inextricably intertwined. The deep cathexis of the "significant other" outstrips clothing, physical appearance and even social condemnation. As one wife told me: "man, woman, it doesn't matter. This is the most beautiful human being I have ever known."

In my work with transsexuals and their spouses, I have observed that many women in these relationships come from previously abusive situations. The transsexual, prior to gender transition, often makes an "ideal" mate. While fitting society's description of how a man looks, they are really feminine and nonthreatening to their spouses. The wives of these men point over and over again to their gentleness, sensitivity and nurturing qualities. The transsexual is a sheep in wolf's clothing.

When Gary first walked through the door that night he had no idea that anything was out of place. Everything seemed exactly the way it had been when he left for work that morning. Of course nothing was the same. As soon as he saw Linda's face he knew that.

The confrontation lasted eight hours. It started with the question: "Are you gay?" and his answer, "No." Linda sat up all night trying to assimilate the towering, indescribable things her husband was telling her. She felt like a constrictor snake who had consumed an animal three times its size and was trying to digest it. But as she lay awake, one thought reverberated in her brain, comforting her in the dark hours of the early morning: the wall was down. There were no more secrets.

So, ironically, the thing that had driven them apart brought them back together. Linda had the old Gary back. Only now he was Glenda. Linda never stopped loving him, and she never would. She went to support groups and in a relatively short period of time, she was leading support groups, trying to help other wives deal with the quagmire of feelings. And Gary, always considerate to a fault, was ever sensitive to Linda. He discussed his plans with her, and elicited her support before implementing them. Electrolysis. Hormones. Surgery.

I am asking Linda if she has had to deal with ridicule and derision by remaining married to Glenda. Her response: "I say that transsexuals are just like any other people. Just because my husband is having an operation to become a woman, he's still the same person. He's just a different gender. I would still love him if he had been in an accident where his penis was accidentally cut off. But this isn't an accident. We're doing it on purpose to make him what he really is."

"Do people ask about your sex life?"

"You bet," she says, matter-of-factly. "That's the first thing they want to know about. There's more to sex than doing it. There's also cuddling, holding and touching. In fact, there are all kinds of ways to have sex. Sometimes we use a dildo. I'm not a lesbian. I married a man, and in my mind's eye, even though she's Glenda, she's still the man I married. It's still the same person."

But Glenda considers herself to be a lesbian. A transsexual lesbian. This is fortunate, in that she is attracted to the person she has always been attracted to — Linda.

"What's the hardest part about this for you?" I ask Linda. "The worst part is that we are often uncomfortable publicly. We can't be affectionate when we are out together. Gary — I mean Glenda, and I like to hold hands. But in public we're perceived as lesbians. New Year's Eve, we went out and when everyone was kissing at midnight we couldn't. We had to wait until we got home before we could kiss one another."

For Gary, the hardest part has been dealing with people who knew him before he transitioned and became Glenda. That is why they have come to see me. To get help in dealing with the almost inevitable losses that accompany this metamorphosis. While the people at work were generally supportive, Gary's family was not. He has had to give up his relationship with his brother, his only sibling, a clergyman, and his seven nieces and nephews.

"Basically, my brother thinks that what I'm doing is 'silly.' That's actually the word he used to describe this, after all the long, heartfelt conversations I had with him, trying to educate and inform him about this condition. My brother told me that if he accepts me for who I am, than that means he's been wrong all his life about having a brother. He just can't rewrite his personal history. He's more concerned with preserving this belief about what I was than actually having a relationship with me. It's very hurtful. He doesn't want any of his children to have contact with me. If it weren't for the incredible love Linda and I have for one another, this would be even harder to bear. It's a big part of the reason that we've decided to leave home and move to another part of the country."

There are two female nurses living, loving, and working somewhere near Clearwater, Florida. One of them always requests to be assigned to the maternity floor. She is never happier at work than when she is holding and caring for a newborn baby. She is taller than the other labor and delivery nurses, but other than that, she is indistinguishable from them. She has never given birth to a child of her own, but she is a grandfather of three. She and her wife Linda are happy. Very happy. Sometimes its true that love conquers all.

DREAM ON

Promptly at 3:15 P.M., Joseph, my eight-year-old, comes bounding into the kitchen leaving a trail of lunchbox, backpack, sweatshirt, gameboy, and other items in a large puddle at the door. Suddenly my kitchen has all the makings of a great garage sale.

"Hi honey, how was school?" I ask.

"Great," he says. Joseph grabs a bag of chips and turns on the TV. End of conversation for 22 minutes plus commercials.

Wednesday night is clinic night in our office, adjacent to the house. My children have grown up watching my husband provide health care and hormones to the transgendered. They like some of our patients, love others, and are polite to all. Last night I witnessed Joseph perform a tiny miracle . . .

Miguel is a twenty year-old Hispanic natal male who lives at home with his mother and two younger siblings. He is a shy, desperately unhappy person who knows that his transsexualism is killing his family. Every time he thinks about his choices, to leave his mother, sister and brother, or take hormones and live alone, he slashes his wrists. I have seen him several times, but his depression is so intractable that we referred him to a psychiatrist and suggested hospitalization. He refused, but calls and cries frequently.

One day I got the call that we (Fred, Samantha, and I) all had been expecting. Miguel had attempted suicide again and his mother had admitted him to a local hospital. When he was discharged, weeks later, it was with the condition that he have an appointment with me and the consulting psychiatrist.

Miguel came to see me and was even worse than before. He was agitated and had taken himself off all antidepressant medications. He refused to see a psychiatrist. He angrily informed me that what he learned in the hospital is that if you try to kill yourself you better succeed. I tried to talk with him but he was wild and flew out of my office. He was gone before I put down my coffee cup.

I phoned the psychiatric hospital, identified myself, and asked them to give me his mother's work phone. "Miguel is intending to harm himself," I told some secretary "and I want to contact his mother immediately." Not, surprisingly they called me back and said he lied about everyone's phone number and they have no accurate information. Great, I thought. That's the last time we'll see him alive.

That night I phoned his mother at home and asked her to come in and talk with me. She arrived the following evening with Miguel in tow. His head was down, his fists clenched, and I realized that I have almost never seen his face. He was always burying himself. He waited while mother and I talked—mother to mother.

"No," she told me, this beautiful proud woman. "I cannot accept this. He will always be my child but he cannot 'change' in my home. I have two other children to consider."

End of story. For a brief moment I considered a career change. Why aren't I selling cosmetics at the new Bloomingdales? I asked myself.

Even though I have failed to impress his mother with the gravity of an imminent suicide, she did concede to go to a support group for parents. I have only gained this ground by reassuring her that her English is "good enough" for her to attend. Small victory.

This Wednesday evening, its a full house. Samantha and Fred are busily examining patients, taking blood chemistries, blood pressures, and writing prescriptions. The patients are waiting patiently in a crowded waiting area. I am counseling one in my office. When I finally emerge I hear, amidst the din, the sweet squeaky voice of Joseph:

"What goes zzub, zzub, zzub?" he asks. "A bee flying backwards." Laughter.

"What do you get if you put ducks in a box?" he asks. "A box of quackers." Laughter.

Puzzled, I peek my head in the kitchen. Joseph is sitting in his pajamas and reading a book of riddles to Miguel. Miguel is smiling. When he does, he is transformed. His face is radiant and his eyes are big, brown, and angelic. He looks like a painting of Jesus on black velvet — the kind they sell on the streets of Mexico.

He catches sight of me and the light vanishes from his features. He is dark once again. I leave them alone and let Joseph work his magic. Tonight I will sleep well. I feel certain that Miguel will not kill himself this night.

Tonight, as I kiss my children good night, they are already fast asleep. I feel the warmth of their necks where I kiss, as they huddle together. Joseph has climbed into bed with his sister, and they lay snuggled like puppies in a litter.

While I don't know what shape their dreams take on this cold, dark night, I know one dream they do not bring forth; the dream that they will wake up as the opposite gender. But I also know, that in beds like this all over the world, some children are sleeping and dreaming that dream, in vain. I hope their parents will be kind to them as their condition unfolds, and they awaken from the unfulfilled dream to the disturbing reality of their gender dysphoria.

I go to sleep and dream of a better world, where there exists true acceptance. But like the young dreamers, I too will have a rude awakening in the morning, when reality descends.

IN MEMORY

Sunday morning. Very early and the phone is ringing. I grope for the phone and wake the child who has sandwiched herself between me and my husband . . .

"Dr. Randi Ettner?"

"Speaking." Bad news coming.

"St. Paul Ramsey Medical Center, in Minnesota." Mind racing. Heart beating.

"We found your card in the wallet of Ruth St. Francis." Pleasant voice. Tentative.

"He was brought in last night with a self-inflicted bullet wound in the head. Death is imminent."

"She," I say, crying.

Ruth Jacqueline St. Francis
1953–1994

AFTERWORD
Listening to Different Voices
Historical Perspective
and Influences

You have just read the stories of contemporary transgendered people who are the patients of a most talented woman, Dr. Randi Cahan Ettner. It is interesting to review the original ten gender patients seen by Dr. Harry Benjamin, who was known as the Father of Transsexualism, and the author of the seminal work, *The Transsexual Phenomenon.* Dr. Benjamin heard old voices giving new utterances to an ancient complaint— to a condition which had prevailed throughout history, but which had precious few tellers, no listeners, and no treatment. Back then, Dr. Benjamin alone listened, and was compelled to journey into a unique new discipline.

Dr. Harry Benjamin made great contributions to the fields of gerontology, endocrinology, and sexology, but he especially exercised his extraordinary influences on the field of gender dysphoria—the area in which he spent the last thirty years of his professional life, from 1948 to his retirement in 1978.

In the later part of Dr. Benjamin's life, my partner and I were honored to be considered his intimate colleagues, and were privileged to receive the complete care of Benjamin's entire gender dysphoria medical files. These files cover a unique practice which began with a singular chance referral from Alfred Kinsey in 1948, to over 1,500 patients. The course and events of Harry Benjamin's professional life unlocked the door to an area of study that would have the most profound implications for our understanding of human nature and that would change the lives of many people forevermore.

When we first gained access to these precious files, we especially wanted to study Benjamin's first patients in order to learn how they described themselves, their feelings, and their lives, before hardly any literature on the subject had been published, even before the phrase "trapped in the wrong body."

Upon reading his first ten cases, we were immediately struck by this realization: that even without any books to read, without any other source of information, with or without childhood conditioning, with or without dystonic families, assuming that he or she was alone and unlike anyone else in the world, Dr. Benjamin's earliest patients came to him self-diagnosed. They described symptoms and conditions exactly as his patients continued to describe themselves throughout his thirty year practice; and exactly as we continue to hear them describe themselves even today. Such descriptions as: the recognition of gender confusion very early in their lives, the attempts at crossdressing, the secrecy, the isolation, the unsuccessful suppression of desires and feelings, and the guilt, mostly the guilt.

Harry Benjamin treated all of these patients as people, and by respectfully listening to each individual voice, he learned from them what gender dysphoria was about. Surely these early patients must be lauded for their courage in seeking a description and a solution for a phenomenon that had as yet no description and no solution. They miraculously discovered a physician who was willing to attempt to treat their unusual condition.

The area of gender dysphoria is a rarity even among rarities, and the mere contemplation of gender shakes most of us to the very foundations of our personalities. When a baby is born, the first question asked: "Is it a boy or a girl?" The answer to this question causes the life-long scripting which creates incongruity and confusion for these individuals.

Dr. Benjamin met Otto, his first patient, in the 1920s. Otto had been secretly crossdressing from early child-hood. Although Otto was not transsexual and would never seek any kind of surgical conversion, he was Dr. Benjamin's entre into the field of gender dysphoria.

Several years later Harry Benjamin was introduced to Alfred Kinsey. The two became good friends, sharing ideas and plans. In 1948, Kinsey was taking sex histories in San Francisco. During one interview, Kinsey was surprised to hear a twenty-three year old boy, Van, express firmly that he wanted to change his sex. Never having heard anything like this, Kinsey referred him to Dr. Benjamin, who was staying in the same hotel. The boy's mother pleaded with Benjamin. "Look at this boy, he's not a boy! You've got to do something to help my son be a girl."

The most fascinating aspect about this very case is that medical people in the United States advised surgery, but due to interference by the Attorney General of Wisconsin and state law interpreting such surgery as mayhem, surgical intervention was prevented.

Through Harry Benjamin's encouragement, Van, now known as Susan, made three trips to Europe, 1953-1958, to complete her operation, which included the construction of a vagina lined with skin of the thigh. She and her mother eventually moved to Canada and were never heard from again.

A year later, in 1949, Kinsey sent Harry Benjamin his third and fourth patient, a most astonishing and extraordinary couple, a female-male and a male-to female transsexual. They married one another twice: the first time in their born gender roles, the second in their reversed roles. A California clinic, trying to locate this couple for a study of legal aspects of name and sex status changes, wrote Harry Benjamin describing them as follows: "..both partners became transvestites; the former husband became legally a man and had the marriage annulled. The pair still live together, however, in reversed roles; the former wife takes the role of husband and breadwinner, and the former husband now stays at home and keeps house."

Barbara and Lauren had already remarried each other by the time Dr. Benjamin met them, and he remained for their entire lives the overseer of their hormone treatment and advisor about all physical and psychological matters. The correspondence with Dr. Benjamin provides much evidence that their marriage was a love affair worthy of a romance novel.

Louise, Harry Benjamin's fifth patient, was an artist who married twice. Louise considered herself a heterosexual transvestite. She reported "vicarious menstruation" that manifested itself in copious nosebleeds that lasted up to three days. Louise felt that society's negative attitude toward crossdressing, in large part, was responsible for her developing two distinct personalities: one for the public to know, and the other—"her true self"—which almost no one knew. By the mid-1950s she wrote: "I consider Louise to be my true identity, even though the birth records say differently, and on this I will stand, for to me, as to most people who know me, I am Louise. I maintain that people are personalities first, and that the statistical facts are merely additional information . . ."

The file on Emory, Dr. Benjamin's sixth patient, was sparse and much of our information was gleaned from Dr. Benjamin's correspondence with Louise. He believed Emory was not a true transsexual, so long as he desired to preserve his male genitals for pleasure. For a long time, Benjamin did not consider anyone a true transsexual unless they would consider sex reassignment surgery in order to have the total body appearance of the opposite, and preferred, gender.

In the early 1950s, Dr. Benjamin wrote Louise, "The papers here are full of the Jorgensen case, the boy that went to Denmark to be operated on, and is now coming back as a girl. I'll probably see the party when she gets home." Mutual friends arranged for Christine and Benjamin to meet, and in April of 1953, the 27-year-old "GI Turned Blonde Bombshell" became Dr. Benjamin's seventh gender dysphoria patient. Although he never made the original diagnosis of her transsexualism, his meeting with "the Jorgensen girl" was the onset of a relationship which lasted his lifetime. Benjamin monitored her hormones and also discussed the multiple problems facing transsexuals.

The most significant feature of Christine Jorgensen's case is not so much the facts of her life, but rather the influence her actions had on the entire world. Christine's surgery affected the gender dysphoric worldwide—providing hope and possible solutions.

Vera came to Dr. Benjamin in 1952, at age 52, the oldest—and ninth— of the original ten patients. She was the only one who had grandchildren. She spent over thirty years seeking out physicians "in hopes of being operated on. Since childhood, I've always had a great desire to be in female attire, and always acted and thought like a female."

Dr. Konrad Van Emde Boaz, an eminent Dutch sexologist, helped Dr. Benjamin arrange Vera's conversion surgery in 1955. She felt she was "the only real true transsexual in the world" because she was the only one who had the courage to complete her operation in three separate stages—castration, peotomy, and vaginoplasty—"the only real way to do this." Even after the surgery, she remained married to her wife, but also took a common-law husband for a while because, she stated, "I need a male to keep my vagina open."

She was a wonderful example of the early success of the operation. Vera considered herself to be the "happiest woman in the world . . . and wouldn't exchange places with any man, even if given a million dollars."

Dr. Benjamin referred to Claire, his tenth patient, as "one of my most interesting cases." Hers was a case of rags to riches, of preoperative misery, and postoperative happiness. Although born male, Claire manifested sufficient anomalies at birth to spend the first thirteen years of her life as a girl, adored by her mother. An accident and subsequent operation revealed her male genetic condition, thus causing Claire untold psychological damage, and the loss of her mother's love. Claire's mother could not accept this "boy monster" whom she once perceived as her "little girl."

With Dr. Benjamin's encouragement, and the inspiration of Christine Jorgensen's story, Claire took a path toward fulfilling her dream. Freed from her livelong gender struggle, her brilliant talent emerged. Claire lived her last twenty-five years in great wealth and contentment. Except for her most intimate friends, no one in her life knew that this loved and wonderful woman was not a genetic female.

It is fascinating to realize how representative these first ten patients were. They were of every combination and complexity known to the gender world, then and now. Can it be a coincidence that the characteristics manifested by all of Dr. Benjamin's first patients, appeared at a very early age, or as far back as they could remember—with or without education, guidance, or conditioning? We do not think so. These characteristics are exactly the same as symptoms and characteristics we hear today. We think that Dr. Benjamin's early patients not only document the initial history of this unique field, but that their stories make an exceptional argument in support of the belief that gender dysphoria is an *in utero* condition.

Dr. Benjamin once wrote that, "Instead of treating the patient, might it not be wiser and more sensible to treat society educationally, so that logic, understanding, and compassion might prevail." We agree. And we hope that the gift that we have been offered—this journey into the lives of gender dysphoric people—will go far to combat the paralyzing guilt and negativity with which this condition is approached by most of the people of the world. Perhaps we can consider that there are more than two possible answers to the question, "Is it a boy or a girl?" That on rare occasions the answer might be neither and both, but instead the answer will be a rare and beautiful combination of boy and girl—another color on the gender rainbow.

Much has changed since Dr. Benjamin saw his first gender patient in 1948. Or has it?

–Leah Cahan Schaefer, Ed.D.
–C. Christine Wheeler, Ph.D.
New York City

BIBLIOGRAPHY

Abramowitz, S. "Psychosocial outcomes of sex reassignment surgery." *Journal of Consulting Clinical Psychology*, 54:183-189, 1986

American Psychiatric Association: *Diagnostic and Statistical Manual of Mental Disorders,* 4th Edition,
Washington, DC, American Psychiatric Association,
1994

Bem, S.L. *The Lenses of Gender: Transforming the
Debate on Sexual Inequality.* New Haven, CT, Yale
University Press, 1993

Benjamin, H. *The Transsexual Phenomenon.* New York,
Julian Press. 1966

Berger, J., Green, R., Laub, D., et al: *Standards of Care:
The Hormonal and Surgical Sex Reassignment of
Gender Dysphoric Persons.* Galveston, TX, University of Texas Medical Branch, Janus Information Center, 1977

Blanchard, R. "The concept of autogynephilia and the topology of male gender dysphoria." *Journal of Nervous and Mental Disorders* 177:616-623, 1989b

Blanchard, R., Steiner, B. *Clinical Management of Gender Identity Disorders in Children and Adults.* Washington, DC, American Psychiatric Press, 1990

Blanchard, R. "The she-male phenomenon and the concept of partial autogynephilia." *Journal of Sex and Marital Therapy* 19 1, 1993

Bockting ,W.O., Coleman, E. "A comprehensive approach to the treatment of gender dysphoria," in *Gender Dysphoria: Interdisciplinary Approaches in Clinical Management.* Edited by Bockting WO, Coleman E. New York, Haworth Press, 1992, pp 131-155

Botzer, M.C., Vehrs, B., Biber, S. "Factors contributing to favorable outcomes of gender reassignment surgery." Paper presented at the 13th International Symposium on Gender Dysphoria, Harry Benjamin International Gender Dysphoria Association, New York, October 1993

Brooks, G., Brown, G. "International survey of 851 transgendered men: the Boulton and Park experience." Paper presented at the Sixth Annual Texas "T" Party, San Antonio, TX, February 26, 1994

Brown, .G.R.. "Bioethical issues in the management of gender dysphoria." *Jefferson Journal of Psychiatry* 6:23-34, 1988a

Brown, G.R. "Transsexuals in the military: flight into hyper-masculinity." *Archives of Sexual Behavior* 17:527-537, 1988b

Brown, G.R. "A review of clinical approaches to gender dysphoria." *Journal of Clinical Psychiatry* 51:57-64, 1990a

Brown, G.R. "The Transvestite Husband." *Medical Aspects of Human Sexuality* 24:35-42, 1990b

Brown,G.R. "106 women in relationships with cross-dressing men: a descriptive study from a non- clinical population." *Archives of Sexual Behavior* 23:515-529, 1994

Cole, C.M., Emory, E.L., Boyle, M., et al: "Comorbidity of gender dysphoria and other major psychiatric diagnoses." Paper presented at the 13th International Symposium on Gender Dysphoria, Harry Benjamin International Gender Dysphoria Association, New York, NY, October 1993

Denny, D. *Current Concepts in Transgender Identity: Towards A New Synthesis.* Garland, [in press]

DiCeglie, D. "Therapeutic aims in working with children and adolescents with gender identity disorders and their families." Paper presented at the 13th International Symposium on Gender Dysphoria, Harry Benjamin International Gender Dysphoria Association, New York, NY, October 1993

Docter, R.F., Fleming, J.S. "Dimensions of transvestism and transsexualism: the validation and factorial structure of the cross-gender questionnaire, in Gender Dysphoria: Interdisciplinary Approaches in Clinical Management." Edited by Bockting WO, Coleman E. New York, Haworth Press, 1992, pp 15-37

Ettner, R. "A workshop model for the inclusion and treatment of the families of transsexuals." Presented at the 14th International Symposium for Gender Dysphoria, Harry Benjamin International Gender Dysphoria Association, Bavaria, Germany, October 1995

Ettner, R., Schacht, M.J., Schrang, E., et al: *Transsexualism: The Phenotype Variable.* 1996 [unpublished]

Garber, M. *Vested Interests: Cross-Dressing and Cultural Anxiety.* New York. Routledge, 1992

Gooren, L. "The endocrinology of transsexualism: A review and commentary." Psychoneuroendocrinology. 1990, Vol. 15, 1 pp3-14

Gottlieb, L.J., Levine, A.L." A new design for the radial forearm free-flap phallic construction." *Plastic Reconstructive Surgery,* 92:276-283, 1993

Gottlieb, L.J., Pielet, R.W., Levine, L.A. "An update on phallic construction," in *Advances in Plastic and Reconstructive Surgery,* Vol 10. Edited by Habal MB New York, Mosby Year Book, 1994, pp267-284

Green, R. *Sexual Identity Conflict in Children and Adults.* New York, Basic Books, 1974

Green, R "One-hundred-ten feminine and masculine boys: behavioral contrasts and demographic similarites." *Archives of Sexual Behavior* 5:425-446, 1976

Green, R. "Sexual differentiation in the human male and female: science, strategies and politics," in *Progress in Sexology.* Edited by Gemme R, Wheeler CC. New York, Plenum, 1977, pp 1-10

Green, R. "Childhood cross-gender behavior and subsequent sexual preference." *American Journal of Psychiatry* 136: 106-108, 1979

Green, R. "Gender identity in childhood and later sexual orientation: follow-up of 78 males." *American Journal of Psychiatry* 136:106-108,1979

Green, R. *The Sissy Boy Syndrome and the Development of Homosexuality.* New Haven, CT, Yale University Press, 1987

Green, R. "Transsexualism and the law." Paper presented at the 13th International Symposium on Gender Dysphoria Harry Benjamin International Gender Dysphoria Association. New York, October l993

Hirschfeld, M. *Die Transvestiten.* Berlin, Pulvermacher, 1910

Ihlenfeld, C.F., Schaefer, L.C., Wheeler, C.C.: *Harry Benjamin, M.D. 1885-1986: The Celebration of a Life.* New York, New York Academy of Medicine, 1987

Jorgensen, C. *Christine Jorgensen [A Personal Autobiography].* New York, Paul S Eriksson, 1967

Kirk, S., Rothblatt, M.A. *Medical, Legal, and Workplace Issues for the Transsexual.* Watertown, MA, Together Lifeworks, 1995

Kirk, S. *Feminizing Hormonal Therapy for the Transgendered.* Watertown, MA, Together Lifeworks, 1996

Kuiper, B., Cohen-Kettenis, P." Sex reassignment surgery: a study of 141 Dutch transsexuals." *Archives of Sexual Behavior* 17:439-457, 1988

Meyer-Bahlburg, H.F.L. "Intersexuality and the diagnosis of gender identity disorder." *Archives of Sexual Behavior* 23:21-40, 1994

Money, J. "The concept of gender identity disorder in childhood and adolescence after 39 years." *Journal of Sex and Marital Therapy* 20:163-177, 1994a

Money, J. *Sex Errors of the Body and Related Syndromes: A Guide to Counseling Children, Adolescents, and Their Families.* Baltimore, MD, Paul H. Brooks, 1994b

Money, J., Ehrhardt, A.A. *Man and Woman, Boy and Girl: The Differentiation and Dimorphism of Gender Identity From Conception to Maturity* Baltimore, MD, Johns Hopkins University Press, 1972

Money, J., Tucker, P. *Sexual Signatures: On Being a Man or a Woman.* Boston, MA, Little, Brown, 1975

Morris, J. *Conundrum.* New York, Harcourt Brace Jovanovich, 1974

Ousterhut, D.K. "Skull modification in the gender dysphoric patient. Paper presented at athe 13th International Symposium on Gender Dysphoria," Harry Benjamin International Gender Dysphoria Association, New York,1993

Pauly, I.B. "Gender identity disorders: evaluation and treatment:" *Journal of Sex Education and Therapy* 16:2-24, 1990

Pauly, I.B. "Terminology and classification of gender

identity disorders, in Gender Dysphoria:" *Interdisciplinary Approaches to Clinical Management.* Edited by Bockting WO, Coleman E. New York, Haworth Press, 1992, pp 1-14

Pfafflin, F. "Unexpected findings of psychologlical testing of pre- and post-operative transsexuals." Paper presented at the 13th International Symposium on Gender Dysphoria, Harry Benjamin International Gender Dysphoria Association, New York, October 1993

Pillard, R.C., Weinrich, J.D." The periodic table of the gender transpositions: a theory based on masculinization and feminization of the brain." *Journal of Sex Research* 23:425-454, 1987

Pleak, R.R., Anderson, D.A. "A parents group for boys with gender identity disorder." Paper presented at the 13th International Symposium on Gender Dysphoria, Harry Benjamin International Gender Dysphoria Association, New York, October 1993

Pomeroy, W.B., Flax, C., Wheeler, C.C.: *Taking a Sex History: Interviewing and Recording.* New York, Free Press, 1982

Richards, R. *Second Serve: The Renee Richards Story.* New York, Stein and Day, 1983

Rothblatt, M.A. *The Apartheid of Sex: A Manifesto on the Freedom of Gender.* New York, Crown, 1995

Rothblatt, M.A. "Transsexual and transgender health law." *Journal of Gender Studies* 15-16 [double issue]: 24-46, 1993-1994

Schaefer, L.C., Wheeler, C.C.: "The non-surgery true transsexual, part II: theoretical rationale." Paper presented at the Ninth International Symposium on Gender Dysphoria, Harry Benjamin International Gender Dysphoria Association, Bordeaux, France, October 1983

Schaefer, L.C., Wheeler, C.C. "Dr. Benjamin's early patients: a perspective." Paper presented at the Ninth International Symposium on Gender Dysphoria, Harry

Benjamin International Gender Dysphoria Association, Minneapolis, MN, October 1985

Schaefer, L.C., Wheeler, C.C. "Harry Benjamin's early cases, 1938-1953: historical influences, part I." Paper presented at the Eighth World Congress for Sexology, Heidelberg, Germany, June, 1987a

Schaefer, L.C., Wheeler, C.C. "Tribute to Harry Benjamin, 1885-1986." Paper presented at the Tenth International Symposium on Gender Dysphoria. Harry Benjamin International Gender Dysphoria Association, Amsterdam, The Netherlands, October 1987b

Schaefer, L.C., Wheeler, C.C. "Guilt and the gender phenomenon." Paper presented at the Eleventh International Symposium on Gender Dysphoria, Harry Benjamin International Gender Dysphoria Association, Cleveland, OH, October 1989

Schaefer, L.C., Wheeler, C.C. "Clinical historical notes: Harry Benjamin's first ten cases [1938-1953]." *Archives of Sexual Behavior* 24:73-93,1995

Schaefer, L.C., Wheeler, C.C. "Guilt and gender identity disorders and condition: understanding, recognizing, diagnosing, and its treatments." *Personal Relationships Journal of the International Society for the Study of Personal Relationships* [in press]

Schaefer, L.C., Wheeler, C.C., Futterweit, W. "Gender identity disorders [transsexualism]" in *Treatment of Psychiatric Disorders,* Vol 2. Washington, DC, American Psychiatric Association, 1995, pp 2015-2079

Stuart, K.E. *The Uninvited Dilemma.* Metamorphous Press, 1983

Sullivan, L. *From Female to Male: The Life of Jack Bee Garland.* Boston, MA, Alyson Publications, 1990

Wheeler, C.C., Schaefer, L.C. "The non-surgery true transsexual-part 1". Paper presented at the Fifth World Congress of Sexology, Jerusalem, Israel, June 1981

Zucker, K.J. "Treatment of gender identity disorders in

children, in Clinical Management of of Gender Identity Disorders in Children and Adults." Edited by Blanchard R, Steiner BW. Washington, DC, American Psychiatric Press, 1990c, pp 27-45

Zucker, K.J., Green, R. "Gender identity disorder of childhood," in *Treatments of Psychiatric Disorders,* Vol.1 Washington, DC, American Psychiatric Association, 1989 pp 661-670

Zucker, K.J., Green, R., Bradley, S., et al "Gender identity disorders of childhood: diagnostic issues," in *DSM-IV Sourcebook.* Edited by Widiger T, Frances A, Pincus H, et al. Washington, DC, American Psychiatric Press, 1995

Zucker, K.J., Bradley, S. *Gender Identity Disorder and Psychosexual Problems in Children and Adolescents.* New York, Guilford Press, 1995

This work was made possible, in part, by a grant from The New Health Foundation, an organization that provides assistance to transgendered people.

Contributions can be made to The New Health Foundation, 1214 Lake Street, Evanston, IL, 60201.